CHINESE CLASSICS

SELECTED READINGS

www.royalcollins.com

CHINESE CLASSICS

SELECTED READINGS

ZHANG TING

Books Beyond Boundaries

ROYAL COLLINS

Chinese Classics: Selected Readings

Zhang Ting

First published in 2022 by Royal Collins Publishing Group Inc.
Groupe Publication Royal Collins Inc.
BKM Royalcollins Publishers Private Limited

Headquarters: 550-555 boul. René-Lévesque O Montréal (Québec) H2Z1B1 Canada
India office: 805 Hemkunt House, 8th Floor, Rajendra Place, New Delhi 110 008

Original Edition © Peking University Press

ISBN: 978-1-4878-0898-3

To find out more about our publications, please visit www.royalcollins.com.

Preface and Acknowledgement

This textbook unfolds the translated Chinese culture in its intellectual history, through the core texts selected from Chinese traditional classics and its critical anthology. It presents the source readings with two formats, the selected classics with its Chinese and English versions paralleled, taking the major role as the close reading materials, and the critical texts in English as the extended readings. Following the major topics of early classics, Confucian, Daoist, and the other schools of thoughts, this textbook makes selections among the most discussed terms, concepts, and motifs in Chinese intellectual history, with an effort to expose the evolution of certain threads of thought throughout. One example is the discussion over the idea of "Junzi," the princely man, as covered in the selections from *The Book of Changes*, *The Analects*, *Mencius*, *Xunzi*, *Dao De Jing*, and *Zhuangzi*.

An editorial feature of this textbook is the paralleled arrangement of the classical texts and their English translations. The texts in two languages abreast make the study of the translation a more convenient step in the learning process. As it turns out, a close-up study on the translation of specific terms or concepts from classical Chinese into modern English has been arousing great interest in my students. So I reckon that for those readers who are well-versed in both languages, this provides great insight into what is lost, created and transformed throughout the translation from classical Chinese to English, while for those who are learning classical Chinese or English, such a textual placement only comes as natural and helpful.

Apart from the readings drawn from classical canons, the extended readings and study questions are devoted to bringing in a part of the critical tradition in the study of Chinese culture, supposedly unrolling a bigger picture of the interpreted classics. Important essays by scholars of Chinese culture or Sinologists are excerpted based on their relevance with the topics in different units, and may sometimes form a dialectical discourse in each unit. Such an arrangement also aims to encourage the students and readers to put up arguments over the perceived traditional culture which is never defined for good but in constant interpretive flux.

To clarify a few teaching-related technicalities, the selected texts come from a rich source in Chinese classical anthologies, and the full bibliographical data can be obtained at the footnotes on the pages of the titles. While considering the Chinese words and names, we believe a Pinyin system is most effective for students in China and learners of Chinese abroad; hence I have rendered those in the Wade-Giles system of Romanization into the official Romanization system for Standard Chinese. Based on a similar rationality, the Chinese names are rendered in their Chinese order, with the family name first and the personal name last. And if any teachers are considering using this textbook in their classes, they may find our online course a good source, and the website is https://moocs.unipus.cn/my/course/1305.

As is quoted, "all the rivers run into the sea, but the sea is not full," the main threads yarned from the different schools of thoughts only run into the sea of Chinese intellectual culture, but never make it full. Though the book only serves as a small dipper in the vastness of the sea, it has shaped into what it is now through a genuine collaboration of colleagues and friends from the following institutions: Professor Zhang Xuchun, Associate Professor Xia Xindong and Associate Professor Wen Yiming from Sichuan International Studies University, Shangguan Qianyi, a former student of SISU who now studies in the graduate school of the University of Macau, and Ms. Liu Wenjing from Peking University Press. Sincere recognition and appreciation are extended to all of them above, for their consistent encouragement and assistance in the planning, organization, reviewing, and editing of this book.

Contents

Chapter 3: Philosophical Daoism and Its Imaginativeness   71

Chapter 4: Chinese Buddhism   105

Chapter 5: The "Others" in Chinese Classics   125

Contents

INTRODUCTION

An Overview of Chinese Culture and Thought

Prehistory

Chinese culture is formed throughout a continuous encountering and integration of varied and diverse regional cultures across the land of China. Since around 7000 years ago, many regional Neolithic and early Bronze Age cultures flourished, bringing forth three cultural groups in the pre-history. They were the confederations of tribes known as Hua Xia along the yellow river, Dong Yi occupying the area of southern Shandong and northern Jiangsu, and Miao Man who lived in today's Hubei, Hunan, and Jiangxi extending to Zhejiang and Guangdong. The coexistence of these early cultures has been substantiated by archeological evidence discovered and interpreted in the 1970s. And such a co-existence could also be figured from the fact that the Three Sovereigns and Five Emperors in early Chinese mythology belonged to different cultural groups.

Though vague and without reliable evidence, the legendary kings represented the ancient Chinese's imagination of their ancestors, especially their early struggling, self-preserving and developing in different regions. Their varied cultural origins might have also contributed to the different accounts of the groupings of these mythological rulers and deities. One account is from the *Records of the Grand Historian*, which identified Heavenly Sovereign, Earthly Sovereign, Tai Sovereign (or Fuxi, Nüwa, Shennong) as the Three Sovereigns, and Yellow Emperor, Zhuanxu, Emperor Ku, Emperor Yao, Shun as the Five Emperors. Among them Shennong, who was also known as Yan Emperor along with Yellow Emperor represented the Hua Xia group, Fuxi and Nüwa the Miao Man confederation. Other primitive cultural heroes included Chi You, who fought against Yellow Emperor and was later subdued by him, and Hou Yi the divine archer, both of whom came from the Dong Yi cultural group.

These cultural heroes, though existed only legendarily in historical texts, became symbols of historical transitions from primitive groups to matriarchal and patriarchal clans, then to tribal groups. The Three Sovereigns were accredited in the early tales as having created mankind or imparted essential knowledge and skills for survival, hence being regarded as gods of the Age of Mythology in ancient China. Philosophical interrogations and explorations of the human-heaven relationship also started during this age, as suggested by the creation of the eight trigrams, legendarily attributed to Fuxi. The Five Emperors, who were known by their supreme morals and leading power, were demigods, with their stories marking the establishment of a patriarchal ruling in the development of family clans to tribal groups, then to confederations of tribal groups, setting the stage for the establishment of the Three Dynasties. Besides, their identities as demigods also suggested the historical continuity from the worship of gods to the worship of human ancestors.

The Three Dynasties
A prevalent worship of gods and deities characterized Shang Dynasty, when state-sponsored ceremonies were frequently held to offer sacrifices to Di, the High God, and natural powers for their divine protection. At the same time, Chinese written language developed with the divinational use of inscriptions on oracle bones and bronze vessels, which were necessities for these religious ceremonies. The rulers during this period were called kings and regarded as speakers and mediators for heavenly gods. They became the highest priest of the state and led the people in state worships, which were done with diviners working with the oracle bones. The dates and locations, the diviners' names, and sometimes the topics were inscribed on the bones made of bovine shoulder bones and turtle plastrons. The divination charges were often directed at ancestors as well as natural powers and the legendary emperors. The charges represented the godly wills on which the royal house based its actions, concerning issues from illness, birth and death, to weather, warfare, agriculture, and so on. After the diviner learned about the cracks on the bones made out of a heating process and gave interpretations, the king occasionally added his readings of the cracks to define the nature of the omen. The mediating role of the king as a communicator with the heavenly gods and ancestors was gradually strengthened when the king became the sole interpreter

of the cracks on the bones in later Shang. The monopolized reading of the oracles by the king implied a diminishing role of the natural power and gods in deciding politics and state affairs when Shang gradually came to an end.

The divination tradition changed after Shang was replaced by Zhou Dynasty, which, though still acknowledged the power of spiritual beings and highly respected "the mandate of heaven," kept the deities at a distance. As claimed by Zhou's historical documents, the Heavenly power was not shown in any other ways but through its moral aspect and only the king who served people's needs could preserve his mandate and the rightful ruling that came with it. The shift of responsibility from heavenly gods to humans called for the Zhou kings to consolidate their governance, and they did so by establishing a feudalist descent line system and the ceremonial institution. The term *de*, which was not found in the oracle bones of Shang, was a key term in many documents of Zhou. And the divination no longer came from mythical revelation from the "Heavenly God" through cracked bones, but from "words of wisdom" as systematized in the form of numbers, yin-and-yang graphs, and prognostic texts in *The Book of Changes* or *I Ching*. The elusive yet inclusive message of this divination text has fascinated thinkers throughout Chinese history and has also shaped the Chinese mind through its variations in different schools of thoughts.

The Spring and Autumn and Warring States Periods
The cultural legacy of Zhou had such a great impact that the Confucian classics were mostly passed down from it. *The Book of Poetry*, *Classic of Documents*, *Book of Rites*, and *Book of Music* were said to have been compiled by Confucius from the materials used as textbooks in official schools of Zhou Dynasty, and *The Book of Changes* was added with commentaries, called Ten Wings, by Confucians, for all its intellectual relevance with Confucian philosophy. And since the Zhou classics were officially compiled and preserved in the form of bamboo-slips bound with warps, they have come to be canonized in Chinese history and called *jing*, i.e. cultural classics.

One of the causes that drove the Confucian ambition to form the Zhou texts into cultural canons is the fact that the society, after Zhou had been brought down by wars between feudal lords, fell into a chaos with battlefields of separatist regimes. No trace of order and harmony could be found as designed by Zhou's feudal system. Confucius and other pre-Qin thinkers tried to devise a rationale for something to replace the bankrupted political institutions. And this gave rise to a grand opportunity for different stratum of the society to speak for their political ideals and propositions, hence the contention of the Hundred Schools of Thought. By criticizing, complementing, counter-arguing each other, the various schools crystallized the myriad voices representing different social status, academic traditions and ways of thinking during the Spring and Autumn and Warring States periods.

It is observed that while Confucianism emphasized social order and active involvement with society, Daoism concentrated on individual life and spiritual transcendence, giving inspiration to the development of Chinese Buddhism and Neo-Confucianism. And different from Confucius who took the Western Zhou as the model and emphasized on humanity and love based on a gradation in human relations, Mozi looked to Xia Dynasty and insisted on righteousness with a preference for universal love without any distinction among familial relations and social rankings. Even the least attractive concern about logic and metaphysics to a traditional Chinese became a central subject matter during this period, taken as the object of discussion for the School of the Logicians. The privately-run school as initiated by Confucius was groundbreaking considering that education had only been accessible to the family of aristocratic officials. It is the flourishing and vivid picture of thoughts during this time that has characterized the periods as the Axial Age in China, bringing into form the Hua Xia civilization that integrates the various regional cultures across the land.

Qin and Han Dynasties

As the old feudal regimes collapsed and were replaced by the centralized monarchy of Qin in 221 BC, its king claimed the title of "First Sovereign Emperor," resuming the title that had only been applied to the demigods in the prehistory legends. The emperor's power was gathered through the extension of the administration system of prefectures and counties and the appointment and dispatch of officials by the central government, the establishment of a network of roads and the defense system, and the standardization of measurements. Along with this reform was the further unification of different fields of culture, including the standardization of the written language and the controlling of varied schools of thoughts. This strong-minded ideological discipline fanned the flame to the already dominating Legalist School, and silenced the other schools by burying the "dangerous and unsettling" intellectuals and their books.

The ideological manipulation found a less violent way into the succeeding empire, Western Han; but this time, it was Confucianism that won the emperor's favor. In the reign of Emperor Wudi, more-intensive political organization and stronger authority of the government were in critical need for the peace and prosperity of the expanding empire. Confucianism, with Dong Zhongshu's interpretive emphasis on its ideas about regulating relationships between people assumed to be positioned in degrees of social rankings, had been gradually adopted as official norms, morals, and ritual and social behavior. Hence Confucian classics were sought-after, reinterpreted, debated over, and widely used in the civil service. This most immediately led to Confucianism's canonical status in Chinese culture. Another change that painted the picture of traditional intellectual culture of China was the Han system of recruiting eligible and meritorious men to staff the civil service of the empire, which laid the foundation for the formation of the regular system of national exam and appointment based upon an education of Confucian classics in Sui and Tang Dynasties.

Wei-Jin Period and Southern and Northern Periods

When Confucianism was wielding its influence mostly in politics and academia in Han, Daoism developed in the mundane and was turned into the native Daoist religion, by combining the Huang Lao cult, the teachings of *The Book of Changes*, the Yin-yang School, astrology, and divination. Daoism, with its teaching of spiritual freedom and enlightenment in nature, lent much inspiration to the art of painting. Meanwhile, with the opening of trade route between China and the West, i.e. the Silk Road, cultural exchanges were more frequent. And this also caused the influx of Buddhism through travelers who had taken the Silk Road from northern India. Chinese Buddhism developed from Han and flourished in the Wei-Jin period, through the translation of Buddhist scriptures and its blending with popular religious beliefs and practices.

It has often been claimed that the warlordism and political turmoil paradoxically provided for the intellectual world a space of freedom to revive the study of ancient classics. Yet the momentum that unleashed the intellectual movement in the chaotic ages had already been found in the bitter controversy between the "Old Text" School and "New Text" School during Han.

The spirit of free intellectual criticism and interrogation, devoid of political vulgarism as in the Confucian scholasticism during Han, characterized the Light Conversation or Pure Conversation and School of Arcane Discourse. The most famous of those indulged in the Light Conversation, the Seven Worthies of the Bamboo Grove, engaged in elegant, carefree, and witty talks and poetry. The School of Arcane Discourse, featuring Wang Bi (226–249), He Yan (d. 249), and Guo Xiang (d. 312), synthesized and extended Confucian and Daoist ideas, applying the mysterious truth of Dao with the intention to review the social and moral philosophy of Confucianism, which set the pattern for the further development of Chinese Buddhism and the revival of Confucianism in Song, in the form of Neo-Confucianism.

Sui, Tang, Song, and Yuan Dynasties

The Sui dynasty (581–618), short-lived yet significant in unifying the country after over three hundred years of division, set the stage for the succeeding Tang dynasty (618–907). The general prosperity of the Tang empire and its extensive ties with the world, accompanied by the state patronage, contributed to the development of Chinese thoughts in full bloom. Philosophical Daoism was canonized. Religious Daoism enjoyed imperial favor and ended up being a state cult through its doctrinal and organizational development, and even when it lost its state patronage in the following dynasties, it still enjoyed popularity among the masses.

The famous pilgrim Xuanzang spoke for the continued imperial favor for Buddhism for most of the dynasty. Most importantly, the development of Buddhist sects during this period raised the subject of consciousness to prominence in Chinese philosophy. Apart from the great project of Buddhist translation led by Xuanzang, indigenous Buddhist schools such as the Tian Tai, Hua Yan, Meditation or Zenism, and Pure Land schools came into being.

If early Buddhist translation could not have won its popularity without its use of Daoist concepts and terms, then the Chinese Buddhist schools would not have rooted into this land without its embracing diverse elements of Chinese culture. The southern Chan (Zen) school gained its anti-textual and anti-metaphysical revelation inspired by Daoist dialectics. And the salvationist preaching of the Pure Land sect incorporated classical ideas to its doctrines.

The tide of Confucian decline during early and mid-Tang was reversed by Han Yu, one of the greatest literary masters who highlighted the Golden Age of culture in Tang and Song, together with Li Ao. They started a Confucian revival, strengthening the Confucian concentration on human nature and social morality against the dominance of Daoism and Buddhism, which became another force that invigorated the Neo-Confucianism or the Learning of the Way.

The gem of Tang culture were undoubtedly its poetry and visual arts, the brilliance of which was carried on into the Song Dynasty (960–1279), despite Song's delicate ruling and weak national power. The fighting with the "barbarian" tribes in the north, say Dangxiang or Tangut, Qidan or Khitan and Nüzhen or Jurchen ended up beefing up the cultural integration of Chinese culture that went all the way into Yuan Dynasty. A wider readership was witnessed with the development of commerce and printing technology, which naturally expanded the education of Confucian classics, based on which the civil service examination continued to sway the bureaucratic staffing. The intellectual center had now shifted from Buddhist temples to regional schools and noted scholars with many followers. One of such scholars was Hu Yuan, whose ideas singled out substance, function and literary expression as the Three Treasures of Confucianism, had a great impact on the Song Confucian classicists as Wang Anshi, Sima Guang, Ouyang Xiu, Fan Zhongyan and Su Dongpo. These classicists were engaged in political applications of Confucian principles to state reforming programs. The most preeminent aspect of the Confucian revival during Song was in metaphysics, known as the School of Principle or Reason and the School of the Mind or Intuition. With inspirations from the Daoist cosmogony and Buddhist quietism and subjectivism, the School of Principle reaffirmed a Confucian tradition that stressed on human values and ethical principles and built them into a universal principle consummated by Zhu Xi (1130–1200). Despite many disputes, Zhu Xi's metaphysics has been well acknowledged by the Far East countries as the most complete expositions of Confucianism.

Ming and Qing Dynasties
After Cheng-Zhu School had been canonized through the civil service examination system in Yuan for over 200 years, it started to lose its vigor in Ming Dynasty (1368–1644), giving way to Wang Yangming's philosophical ideas representing the School of the Mind. Wang Yangming's intuitionism attracted many thinkers in late Ming, but also anticipated, together with Cheng-Zhu school, a reaction against speculative philosophy and a resuming of the practical side of Confucianism, especially its use in political affairs. The Donglin Academy was such a group that directed its contention against the corrupt Ming governance and called for a moral regeneration of the ruling class by going back to Confucian ethics.

The call had not been established upon a historical profundity and broadness until Huang Zongxi and Gu Yanwu, who were regarded as two of the Three Great Confucians in late Ming and early Qing. They attempted to reverse the trend of empty speculation in the School of Mind and the rigidity with formality and scholasticism as developed from the School of Principle in late Ming intelligentsia. In a certain sense, the leaning toward practicality and objective truth in the Confucian studies came under the influence of western knowledge introduced by Jesuits, who brought with them the scientific revolution. The third one of the Great Confucians was Wang Fuzhi, whose earlier failure in resisting the Manchu rule had most probably formed his strong sense of racial consciousness and culture preservation in his reapplication of Confucian ideas. He rejected the transcendental principle (li) upheld by Neo-Confucianism and took on a more materialistic approach by emphasizing the integrated existence of the material force (qi) and the concrete object with its specific principle inherent. From a cyclical view of material force as being involved in constant fusion and intermingling and thus of principles kept being renewed, Wang Fuzhi rejected the Confucian look-back upon the past as the model for today, which further determined his denial of Zhou feudalism.

Despite the early signs of enlightenment as shown in the practical Confucianism, the possibility of a more open and unbarred intellectual engagement was more or less stifled by the centralized despotism and literary censorship during Ming and Qing. This turned many scholars in Qing from politics to the Empirical School of Scholarship, also named as Qian Jia School which focused on verifying the authenticity of classical texts, questioning the canonized ones, challenging the Neo-Confucian orthodoxy. Influence of European mathematics and mathematical astrology should be credited in this trend of study. During both Ming and Qing, the pride that the imperial authorities enjoyed from a stable, prosperous society and far-reaching international impact fueled the national project of compiling cultural heritage in huge anthologies and encyclopedias. This also set an example for the private endeavor of book publishing and library building in the literati. The most famous among the great works that have preserved the legacy of Chinese intellectual culture were the *Great Canon of the Yongle Era, Index of Native Herbs, Treatise on Military Preparedness, Creations of Heaven and Human Labor* in Ming, and *Kangxi Dictionary, Complete Library of the Four Treasuries, Rime Storehouse of Esteemed Phrases* and *Exegesis of Confucian Classics*.

Timeline of Chinese Culture and Thought

Qin 秦   221 BC–206 BC
Han 汉   206 BC–220 AD

    Western Han 西汉 206 BC–25 AD
    Xin 新 (Wang Mang 王莽 reign) 9–23
    Eastern Han 东汉 25–220

Wei, Jin, Nan-Bei Chao 魏晋南北朝   220–589

    Sanguo 三国 (Three Kingdoms) 220–280
    Wei 魏 (commonly known as Cao Wei 曹魏) 220–265
    Han 汉 (commonly known as Shu Han 蜀汉) 221–263
    Wu 吴 (commonly known as Sun Wu 孙吴) 222–280
    Jin 晋 265–420
    Western Jin 西晋 265–317
    Eastern Jin 东晋 317–420
    Six Dynasties 六朝 222–589
    Sixteen Kingdoms 十六国 304–439

Nan-Bei Chao 南北朝 420–589
(Northern and Southern Dynasties)

Southern Dynasties 南朝 420–589
Liu Song 刘宋 420–479
Qi 齐 479–502
Liang 梁 502–557
Chen 陈 557–589

Northern Dynasties 北朝 386–581
Northern Wei 北魏 386–534
Eastern Wei 东魏 534–550
Western Wei 西魏 535–556
Northern Qi 北齐 550–577
Northern Zhou 北周 557–581

Sui 隋   581–618
Tang 唐   618–907
Wudai Shiguo 五代十国   907–960
(The Five Dynasties and Ten Kingdoms)

Five Dynasties 五代(North China) 907–960
Ten Kingdoms 十国(South China) 902–979

Song 宋   960–1279

Northern Song 北宋 period 960–1127
Southern Song 南宋 period 1127–1279

Liao 辽(Qidan 契丹, Khitan)   907–1125
Jin 金(Nüzhen 女真, Jurchen)   1115–1234
Xia 夏 [Xixia 西夏] (Dangxiang 党项, Tangut)   1038–1227
Yuan 元 (Menggu 蒙古, Mongol)   1206–1368
Ming 明   1368–1644
Qing 清 (Manzhou 满洲, Manchu)   1616–1911

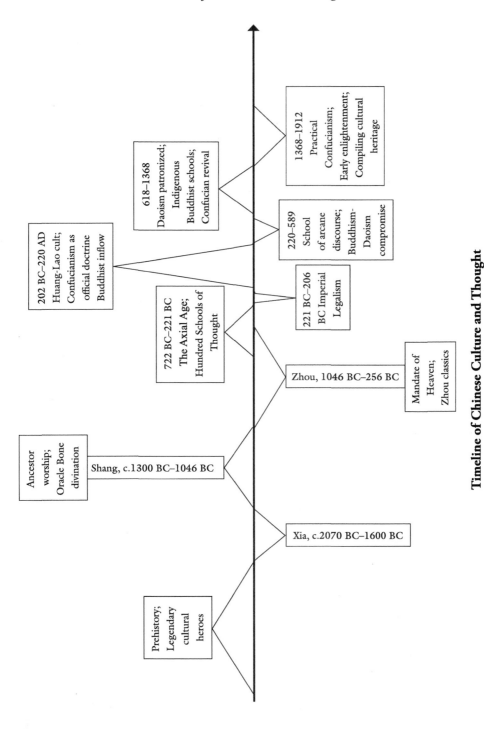

Timeline of Chinese Culture and Thought

Prehistory; Legendary cultural heroes

Xia, c.2070 BC–1600 BC

Ancestor worship; Oracle Bone divination

Shang, c.1300 BC–1046 BC

Zhou, 1046 BC–256 BC

Mandate of Heaven; Zhou classics

722 BC–221 BC The Axial Age; Hundred Schools of Thought

221 BC–206 BC Imperial Legalism

202 BC–220 AD Huang-Lao cult; Confucianism as official doctrine Buddhist inflow

220–589 School of arcane discourse; Buddhism-Daoism compromise

618–1368 Daoism patronized; Indigenous Buddhist schools; Confucian revival

1368–1912 Practical Confucianism; Early enlightenment; Compiling cultural heritage

CHAPTER ❶

Spatial and Temporal Ideas of Early Chinese Culture

1. As we see from one of the earliest cultural texts, *I Ching*, or *The Book of Changes*, dragon functions as the subject of development. And legendary heroes as Nüwa and Fuxi, along with Yellow Emperor were all related to the image of dragon. How does it relate to the fact that we call ourselves the Descendent of Dragon?
2. At the request of Emperor Wanli in Ming Dynasty, the famous Italian missionary Matteo Ricci composed the first European-style map of the world in Chinese, making China at the center of the map. Why did he put China right at the center of the globe?
3. Can you recall any of Chinese Emperors' moving of the capitals in history? What are the usual reasons and routes of the moving? What rituals can you imagine were involved before, during and after the actual moving of the capitals?

Introduction

When we talk about "traditional Chinese culture," we bear in mind the culturally changing yet timeless elements of the culture, since what we regard as the traditions have passed along history and survived into our world for the fact that they have defined our cultural identity. Texts from history are one type of such traditions. In seeking for the origins of the Chinese culture, we find among the earliest texts those canonized through Chinese scholars' illuminations and interpretations of the most basic concepts about time and space, the two of which being basically what we believe to have structured the world we live in. They have become one kind in our cultural legacy that has characterized the "Chinese mind" to understand the universe and human society.

One set of the early texts that are illustrative of the early "Chinese mind" are the sixty-four hexagrams in various combinations of six grams/lines either of yin (the feminine, negative principle, the number of six) or yang (the masculine, initiating principle, the number of nine) principle, which were recognized as divined symbols, depicting the interacting among the earth (the two lines at the bottom), the human (the two lines in the middle), and the heaven (the two lines on the top). As it were, the hexagrams in *I Ching*, or *The Book of Changes*, have been texts of signs that directed the ancient people to certain choices and actions in the world. This sense of locality is found everywhere in the book, which was mostly used for divination, reminding people that their placement in a certain social status and life was permanently changing, and to remain steadfast was to keep being adapted with the changing time and positions. And the one lesson that did not change was the fact that one should remain in the center, the middle course, or the Doctrine of the Mean when the yin and yang merged with each other, because if not, when the yin form went to an end, the extremity would turn it over to the other extremity of the yang form and produce unexpected results. This cyclical sense of time also grounded the sexagenary cycle of recording days and time, designated by combinations of the ten heavenly stems and twelve earthly branches. And the desire to avoid unexpected transformations between yin and yang has also led to a Chinese romance with the word, "the middle," the very name of the country, and foreshadows later dynasties' relentless efforts to place their political and economic center at the heart of the land, the Central Plain, and their self-identification as the world center for centuries to come.

The first two hexagrams of *I Ching* excerpted as the first selection of the chapter present the very basic of Chinese philosophical mind-set, one that conceptualizes the varied moments and positions in life between the heaven and earth. And the second text "The Announcement of The Duke of Shao" from the *Classic of Documents* serves as an example showing how a kingdom determined to move its capital based on the early conceptualization of time and space at a critical moment of its fate.

Selected Passages from *The Book of Changes*[1]

《易经》选篇

Qian: The Creative

The Creative works sublime success, furthering through perseverance: sublimity, potentiality of success, power to further, perseverance.

乾：

元，亨，利，贞。

Nine at the beginning means:

Hidden dragon. Do not act.

初九：潜龙，勿用。

Nine in the second place means:

Dragon appearing in the field. It furthers one to see the great man.

九二：见龙在田，利见大人。

Nine in the third place means:

All day long the superior man is creatively active. At nightfall his mind is still beset with cares. Danger. No blame.

九三：君子终日乾乾，夕惕若。厉无咎。

Nine in the fourth place means: Wavering flight over the depths. No blame.

九四：或跃在渊，无咎。

Nine in the fifth place means: Flying dragon in the heavens. It furthers one to see the great man.

九五：飞龙在天，利见大人。

Nine at the top means: Arrogant dragon will have cause to repent.

上九：亢龙，有悔。

When all the lines are nines, it means:

There appears a flight of dragons without heads. Good fortune.

用九：见群龙无首，吉。

The Image: Heaven moves forever vigorously, likewise, a superior man strives on his own initiative constantly.

《象》曰：天行健，君子以自强不息。

"Hidden dragon. Do not act," it means that yang qi just begins to stir at the lowest place.

"潜龙勿用"，阳在下也。

"Dragon appearing in the field," it means that the great man has extended his virtue far and wide.

"见龙在田"，德施普也。

"All day long the superior man is creatively active," it

"终日乾乾"，反复道也。

---

1. Wilhelm, Richard, Cary F. Baynes (trans.), *I Ching: Or, Book of Changes,* (3rd. ed.), Bollingen Series XIX, Princeton NJ: Princeton University Press, 1967. The image translation of Qian is partly adapted from Fu, Huisheng, *The Zhou Book of Change*, Vol. One, Changsha: Hunan People's Publishing House, 2008, p. 5.

means that he perseveres in the right way time and again.

"Wavering flight over the depths," it means that the great man advances or retreats timely.

"Flying dragon in the heavens," it means that the great man is developing into his cause.

"Arrogant dragon will have cause to repent," it means that he cannot stay long in his prime.

"There appears a flight of dragons without heads," it means that the virtue of heaven is not to pose as the leader.

Kun: The Receptive

The Receptive brings about sublime success, furthering through the perseverance of a mare. If the superior man undertakes something and tries to lead, he goes astray; but if he follows, he finds guidance. It is favorable to find friends in the west and south, to forego friends in the east and north. Quiet perseverance brings good fortune.

Six at the beginning means: When there is hoarfrost underfoot, solid ice is not far off.

Six in the second place means: Straight, square, great. Without purpose, yet nothing remains unfurthered.

Six in the third place means: Hidden lines. One is able to remain persevering.

If by chance you are in the service of a king, seek not works, but bring to completion.

Six in the fourth place means: A tied-up sack. No blame, no praise.

Six in the fifth place means: A yellow lower garment[1] brings supreme good fortune.

Six at the top means: Dragons fight in the meadow. Their blood is black and yellow.

When all the lines are sixes, it means: Lasting perseverance furthers.

The Image: The earth's condition is receptive devotion.

"或跃在渊"，进无咎也。

"飞龙在天"，大人造也。

"亢龙有悔"，盈不可久也。

"用九"，天德不可为首也。

坤：

元亨。利牝马之贞。君子有攸往，先迷，后得主，利。西南得朋，东北丧朋。安贞吉。

初六：履霜，坚冰至。

六二，直、方、大，不习，无不利。

六三，含章，可贞。或从王事，无成有终。

六四，括囊，无咎无誉。

六五，黄裳，元吉。

上六，龙战于野，其血玄黄。

用六，利永贞。

《象》曰：地势坤。君子以厚德载物。

---

1. In the class-based society of ancient times, the formal attire of a scholar was a black robe with a yellow lower garment. The robe was long and covered the yellow garment. Humility is of an inner beauty, like the beauty of the yellow garment covered by the black robe.

Thus the superior man, who has breadth of character, carries the outer world.

When the first hoarfrost comes in the autumn, the power of darkness and cold is just at its beginning. After these first warnings, signs of death will gradually multiply, until, in obedience to immutable laws, stark winter with its ice is here.

Nature creates all beings without erring: this is its foursquareness. It tolerates all creatures equally: this is its greatness. Therefore it attains what is right for all without artifice or special intentions.

If a man is free of vanity he is able to conceal his abilities and keep them from attracting attention too soon; thus he can mature undisturbed.

The time is dangerous, because any degree of prominence leads either to the enmity of irresistible antagonists if one challenges them or to misconceived recognition if one is complaisant. Therefore a man ought to maintain reserve, be it in solitude or in the turmoil of the world, for there too he can hide himself so well that no one knows him.

Yellow is the color of the earth and of the middle; it is the symbol of that which is reliable and genuine.

If it attempts to maintain a position to which it is not entitled and to rule instead of serving, it draws down upon itself the anger of the strong. A struggle ensues in which it is overthrown, with injury, however, to both sides. The dragon, symbol of heaven, comes to fight the false dragon that symbolized the inflation of the earth principle. Midnight blue is the color of heaven; yellow is the color of earth. Therefore, when black and yellow blood flow, it is a sign that in this unnatural contest both primal powers suffer injury.

When nothing but sixes appears, the hexagram of the Receptive changes into the hexagram of the Creative. By holding fast to what is right, it gains the power of enduring. There is indeed no advance, but neither is there retrogression.

"履霜坚冰"，阴始凝也，驯致其道，至坚冰也。

六二之动，直以方也。"不习无不利"，地道光也。

"含章可贞"，以时发也。"或从王事"，知光大也。
"括囊无咎"，慎不害也。

"黄裳元吉"，文在中也。
"龙战于野"，共道穷也。

用六"永贞"，以大终也。

"The Announcement of the Duke of Shao" from *The Classic of Documents*[1]

《尚书·召诰》选篇

King Cheng, being in Feng and wishing to fix his residence at Luo, sent the Duke of Shao ahead to survey the locality. Thus was made "the Announcement to the Duke of Shao."[2]

In the second month, third quarter, sixth day yi-wei, the king in the morning proceeded from Zhou and arrived in Feng.

The Grand Guardian, the Duke of Shao, preceded the Duke of Zhou to inspect the site. In the third month, the day mu-shen, the third day after the first appearance of the new moon on bing-wu, the Grand Guardian arrived in the morning at Luo and consulted the tortoise oracle about the site.

When he had obtained the oracle he planned and laid out the city.

On the third day geng-xu, the Grand Guardian with all the Yin people started work on the emplacements at the bend of the Luo River, and on the fifth day jia-yin the emplacements were determined.

The next day yi-mao, the Duke of Zhou arrived in the morning at Luo and thoroughly inspected the plans for the new city.

On the third day ding-si, he sacrificed two oxen as victims on the suburban altar, and on the next day mao-wu he sacrificed to the God of the Soil in the new city one ox, one sheep, and one pig.

成王在丰，欲宅洛邑，使召公先相宅，作《召诰》。

惟二月既望，越六日乙未，王朝步自周，则至于丰。

惟太保先周公相宅，越若来三月，惟丙午朏。越三日戊申，太保朝至于洛，卜宅。

厥既得卜，则经营。

越三日庚戌，太保乃以庶殷攻位于洛汭f。越五日甲寅，位成。

若翼日乙卯，周公朝至于洛，则达观于新邑营。

越三日丁巳，用牲于郊，牛二。越翼日戊午，乃社于新邑，牛一，羊一，豕一。

---

1. Wm Theodore de Bary, Wing-Tsit Chan, and Burton Watson, *Sources of Chinese Tradition*, NY: Columbia University Press, 1960.
2. King Cheng, at this time still very young, was the third king of the Zhou dynasty and the second to actually reign. The Duke of Shao and the Duke of Zhou were his chief advisers. It was at this time that the capital of the Zhou state was first fixed at the city of Luo.

On the seventh day jia-zi the Duke of Zhou by written documents gave charges to all the rulers of the states of the Hou, Dian, and Nan zones in the Yin realm. When orders have been given to the Yin multitude they arose with vigor to do their work.

The Grand Guardian then together with all the ruling princes of the states went out and took gifts and entered again and gave them to the Duke of Zhou. The Duke of Shao said: "I salute and bow down my head and I extol the king and your Grace. I make an announcement to all Yin and managers of affairs. Oh, august Heaven, the Lord-on-High, has changed his principal son [i.e. the ruler] and this great state Yin's mandate. Now that the king has received the mandate, unbounded is the grace, but also unbounded is the solicitude.

Oh, how can he be but careful! Heaven has removed and made an end to the great state Yin's mandate. There are many former wise kings of Yin in Heaven, and the later kings and people here managed their mandate. But in the end [under the last king] wise and good men lived in misery so that, leading their wives and carrying their children, wailing and calling to Heaven, they went to where no one could come and seize them.

Oh, Heaven had pity on the people of the four quarters, and looking with affection and giving its mandate, it employed the zealous ones [i.e. the leaders of the Zhou]. May the king now urgently pay careful attention to his virtue.

Look at the ancient predecessors, the lords of Xia; Heaven indulged them and cherished and protected them. They strove to comprehend the obedience to Heaven; but in these times they neglect the aged elders. ...

Now a young son is the successor; may he not have lost their mandate. Then he will comprehend our ancient men's virtue, nay still more it will occur that he is able to comprehend and endeavor to follow Heaven? ...

May the king come and take over the work of the Lord-on High, and himself manage the government in the center of the land. Dan says: 'having made the great city,

越七日甲子，周公乃朝用书命庶殷侯甸男邦伯。厥既命殷庶，庶殷丕作。

太保乃以庶邦冢君出取币，乃复入锡周公。曰："拜手稽首，旅王若公诰告庶殷越自乃御事：呜呼！皇天上帝，改厥元子兹大国殷之命。惟王受命，无疆惟休，亦无疆惟恤。

呜呼！曷其奈何弗敬？天既遐终大邦殷之命，兹殷多先哲王在天，越厥后王后民，兹服厥命。厥终，智藏癏在。夫知保抱携持厥妇子，以哀吁天，徂厥亡，出执。

呜呼！天亦哀于四方民，其眷命用懋。王其疾敬德！

相古先民有夏，天迪从子保，面稽天若；今时既坠厥命。……

今冲子嗣，则无遗寿耇，曰其稽我古人之德，矧曰其有能稽谋自天？……

王来绍上帝，自服于土中。曰：'其作大邑，其自时配皇天，毖祀于上

he shall from here be a counterpart to august Heaven. He shall carefully sacrifice to the upper and lower spirits, and from here centrally govern; and then the King could follow the mandate to rule." ...

We should not fail to mirror ourselves in the lords of Xia; we likewise should not fail to mirror ourselves in the lords of Yin. We do not presume to know and say that the lords of Xia undertook Heaven's mandate so as to have it for so-and-so many years; we do not presume to know and say that it could not have been prolonged. It was that they did not reverently attend to their virtue, and so they prematurely renounced their mandate.

We do not presume to know and say that the lords of Yin received Heaven's mandate. We do not presume to know and say that the lords of Yin received Heaven's mandate for so-and-so many years; we do not know and say that it could not have been prolonged. It was that they did not reverently attend to their virtue and so they prematurely threw away their mandate.

Now the king has succeeded to and received their mandate. We should then also remember the mandates of these two states and in succeeding to them equal their merits. ...

Being king, his position will be that of a leader in virtue; the small people will then imitate him in all the world. ... May those above and below [i.e., the king and his servants] labor and be anxiously careful; may they say: we have received Heaven's mandate, may it grandly equal the span of years of the Lords of Xia and not miss the span of years of the lords of Yin."

下，其自时中乂；王厥有成命治民'。……

我不可不监于有夏，亦不可不监于有殷。我不敢知曰，有夏服天命，惟有历年；我不敢知曰，不其延。惟不敬厥德，乃早坠厥命。

我不敢知曰，有殷受天命，惟有历年；我不敢知曰，不其延。惟不敬厥德，乃早坠厥命。

今王嗣受厥命，我亦惟兹二国命，嗣若功。……

其惟王位在德元，小民乃惟刑用于天下，越王显。上下勤恤，其曰我受天命，丕若有夏历年，式勿替有殷历年。欲王以小民受天永命。"

Extensive Reading A

Foreword to *I Ching*[1]

Carl Gustav Jung

The Chinese mind, as I see it at work in the *I Ching*, seems to be exclusively preoccupied with the chance aspect of events. What we call coincidence seems to be the chief concern of this peculiar mind, and what we worship as causality passes almost unnoticed. We must admit that there is something to be said for the immense importance of chance. An incalculable amount of human effort is directed to combating and restricting the nuisance or danger represented by chance. Theoretical considerations of cause and effect often look pale and dusty in comparison to the practical results of chance. It is all very well to say that the crystal of quartz is a hexagonal prism. The statement is quite true in so far as an ideal crystal is envisaged. But in nature one finds no two crystals exactly alike, although all are unmistakably hexagonal. The actual form, however, seems to appeal more to the Chinese sage than the ideal one. The jumble of natural laws constituting empirical reality holds more significance for him than a causal explanation of events that, moreover, must usually be separated from one another in order to be properly dealt with.

The manner in which the *I Ching* tends to look upon reality seems to disfavor our causalistic procedures. The moment under actual observation appears to the ancient Chinese view more of a chance hit than a clearly defined result of concurring causal chain processes. The matter of interest seems to be the configuration formed by chance events in the moment of observation, and not at all the hypothetical reasons that seemingly account for the coincidence. While the Western mind carefully sifts, weighs, selects, classifies, isolates, the Chinese picture of the moment encompasses everything down to the minutest nonsensical detail, because all of the ingredients make up the observed moment.

Thus it happens that when one throws the three coins, or counts through the forty-nine yarrow stalks, these chance details enter into the picture of the moment of observation and form a part of it—a part that is insignificant to us, yet

---

1. Richard Wilhelm, Cary F. Baynes (trans.), *I Ching: Or, Book of Changes*, (3rd. ed.), Bollingen Series XIX. Princeton: Princeton University Press, 1967.

most meaningful to the Chinese mind. With us it would be a banal and almost meaningless statement (at least on the face of it) to say that whatever happens in a given moment possesses inevitably the quality peculiar to that moment. This is not an abstract argument but a very practical one. There are certain connoisseurs who can tell you merely from the appearance, taste, and behavior of a wine the site of its vineyard and the year of its origin. There are antiquarians who with almost uncanny accuracy will name the time and place of origin and the maker of an object d'art or piece of furniture on merely looking at it. And there are even astrologers who can tell you, without any previous knowledge of your nativity, what the position of sun and moon was and what zodiacal sign rose above the horizon in the moment of your birth. In the face of such facts, it must be admitted that moments can leave long-lasting traces.

In other words, whoever invented the *I Ching* was convinced that the hexagram worked out in a certain moment coincided with the latter in quality no less than in time. To him the hexagram was the exponent of the moment in which it was cast—even more so than the hours of the clock or the divisions of the calendar could be—inasmuch as the hexagram was understood to be an indicator of the essential situation prevailing in the moment of its origin.

This assumption involves a certain curious principle that I have termed synchronicity[1], a concept that formulates a point of view diametrically opposed to that of causality. Since the latter is a merely statistical truth and not absolute, it is a sort of working hypothesis of how events evolve one out of another, whereas synchronicity takes the coincidence of events in space and time as meaning something more than mere chance, namely, a peculiar interdependence of objective events among themselves as well as with the subjective (psychic) states of the observer or observers.

The ancient Chinese mind contemplates the cosmos in a way comparable to that of the modern physicist, who cannot deny that his model of the world is a decidedly psychophysical structure. The microphysical event includes the observer just as much as the reality underlying the *I Ching* comprises subjective, i.e. psychic conditions in the totality of the momentary situation. Just as causality describes the sequence of events, so synchronicity to the Chinese mind deals with the coincidence of events. The causal point of view tells us a dramatic story about how D came into existence: it took its origin from C, which existed before D, and C in its turn had a father, B, etc. The synchronistic view on the other hand tries to produce an equally meaningful picture of coincidence. How does it happen

---

1. "Synchronicity: An Acausal Connecting Principle," *The Structure and Dynamics of the Psyche*, Coll. Works of C. G. Jung, vol. 8.

that A', B', C', D', etc., appear all in the same moment and in the same place? It happens in the first place because the physical events A' and B' are of the same quality as the psychic events C' and D', and further because all are the exponents of one and the same momentary situation. The situation is assumed to represent a legible or understandable picture.

Now the sixty-four hexagrams of the *I Ching* are the instrument by which the meaning of sixty-four different yet typical situations can be determined. These interpretations are equivalent to causal explanations. Causal connection is statistically necessary and can therefore be subjected to experiment. Inasmuch as situations are unique and cannot be repeated, experimenting with synchronicity seems to be impossible under ordinary conditions[1]. In the *I Ching*, the only criterion of the validity of synchronicity is the observer's opinion that the text of the hexagram amounts to a true rendering of his psychic condition. It is assumed that the fall of the coins or the result of the division of the bundle of yarrow stalks is what it necessarily must be in a given "situation," inasmuch as anything happening in that moment belongs to it as an indispensable part of the picture. If a handful of matches is thrown to the floor, they form the pattern characteristic of that moment. But such an obvious truth as this reveals its meaningful nature only if it is possible to read the pattern and to verify its interpretation, partly by the observer's knowledge of the subjective and objective situation, partly by the character of subsequent events. It is obviously not a procedure that appeals to a critical mind used to experimental verification of facts or to factual evidence. But for someone who likes to look at the world at the angle from which ancient China saw it, the *I Ching* may have some attraction.

---

1. J. B. Rhine, *The Reach of the Mind*, New York and London: 1928.

Geographic Background of the Chinese People[1]

Feng Youlan

In the *Confucian Analects* Confucius said: "The wise man delights in water; the good man delights in mountains. The wise move; the good stay still. The wise are happy; the good endure." In reading this saying, I feel there is in it something which suggests a difference between the people of ancient China and those of ancient Greece.

China is a continental country. To the ancient Chinese their land was the world. There are two expressions in the Chinese language which can both be translated as the world. One is "all beneath the sky" and the other is "all within the four seas." To the people of a maritime country such as the Greeks, it would be inconceivable that expressions such as these could be synonymous. But that is what happens in the Chinese language, and it is not without reason.

From the time of Confucius until the end of the last century, no Chinese thinkers had the experience of venturing out upon the high seas. Confucius and Mencius lived not far from the sea, if we think in modern terms of distance, yet in the *Analects*, Confucius mentions the sea only once. He is recorded as saying: "If my way is not to prevail I shall get upon a raft and float out to the sea. He who will go with me will be [Zhong] You." Zhong You was a disciple of Confucius's known for his courage and bravery. It is said in the same work that when Zhong You heard this statement, he was much pleased. Confucius, however, was not so pleased by Zhong You's overenthusiasm, and remarked: "You is braver than myself, I do not know what to do with him."

Mencius's reference to the sea is likewise brief. "He who has seen the sea," he says, "finds it difficult to think anything about other waters; and he who has wandered to the gate of the sage, finds it difficult to think anything about the words of others." Mencius is no better than Confucius, who thought only of "floating out to the sea." How different were Socrates, Plato, and Aristotle, who lived in a maritime country and wandered from island to island!

---

1.   Feng, Youlan, *A Short History of Chinese Philosophy*, New York: The Free Press, 1948.

Maritime Countries and Continental Countries

The Greeks lived in a maritime country and maintained their prosperity through commerce. They were primarily merchants. And what merchants have to deal with first are the abstract numbers used in their commercial accounts, and only then with concrete things that may be immediately apprehended through these numbers. Such numbers are what Northrop called concepts by postulation; Hence Greek philosophers likewise took the concept by postulation as their starting point. They developed mathematics and mathematical reasoning. That is why they had epistemological problems and why their language was so articulate.

But merchants are also townsmen. Their activities demand that they live together in towns. Hence they have a form of social organization not based on the common interest of the family so much as on that of the town. This is the reason why the Greeks organized their society around the city state, in contrast with the Chinese social system, which may be called that of the family state because under it the state is conceived of in terms of the family. In a city state the social organization is not automatic, because among the same class of townsmen, there is no moral reason why one should be more important than, or superior to, another. But in a family state, the social organization is automatic and hierarchic because in a family the authority of the father is naturally superior to that of the son.

The fact that the Chinese were farmers also explains why China failed to have an industrial revolution, which is instrumental for the introduction of the modern world. In the *Liezi* there is a story which says that the Prince of the State of Song once asked a clever artisan to carve a piece of jade into the leaf of a tree. After three years the artisan completed it, and when the artificial leaf was put upon the tree, it was made so wonderfully that no one could distinguish it from the real leaves. Thereupon the Prince was much pleased. But when Liezi heard it, he said: "If nature took three years to produce one leaf; there would be few trees with leaves on them!" (*Liezi* ch. 8.) This is the view of one who admires the natural and condemns the artificial, and in their primitivity and innocence, they are easily made content. They desire no change nor can they conceive of any change. In China there have been not a few notable inventions or discoveries, but we often find that these were discouraged rather than encouraged.

With the merchants of a maritime country conditions are otherwise. They have greater opportunity to see different people with different customs and different languages; they are accustomed to change and are not afraid of novelty. Nay, in order to have a good sale for their goods they have to encourage novelty in the manufacture of what they are going to sell. It is no accident that in the West, the industrial revolution was first started in England, which is also a maritime country maintaining her prosperity through commerce.

What was quoted earlier in this chapter from the *Lü Shi Chun Qiu* about merchants can also be said of the people of maritime countries, provided that, instead of saying that they are corrupt and treacherous, we say that they are refined and intelligent. We can also paraphrase Confucius by saying that the people of maritime countries are the wise, while those of continental countries are the good. And so we repeat what Confucius said: "The wise delight in water; the good delight in mountains." The wise move; the good stay still. The wise are happy; the good endure.

Extensive Reading C

North and South[1]

Lin Yutang

The common historical tradition, the written language, which has in a singular way solved the problem of Esperanto in China, and the cultural homogeneity achieved through centuries of slow, peaceful penetration of a civilization over comparatively docile aborigines, have achieved for China the basis of the common brotherhood so much desirable now in Europe. Even the spoken language presents no difficulty nearly so great as confronts Europe today. A native of Manchuria can, with some difficulty, make himself understood in southwest Yunnan, a linguistic feat made possible by a slow colonization process and helped greatly by the system of writing, the visible symbol of China's unity.

This cultural homogeneity sometimes makes us forget that racial differences, differences of blood, do exist within the country. At close range the abstract notion of a Chinaman disappears and breaks up into a picture of a variety of races, different in their stature, temperament and mental make-up. It is only when we try to put a southern commander over northern soldiers that we are abruptly reminded of the existing differences. For on the one hand we have the northern Chinese, acclimatized to simple thinking and hard living, tall and stalwart, hale, hearty and humorous, onion-eating and fun-loving, children of nature, who are in every way more Mongolic and more conservative than the conglomeration of peoples near Shanghai and who suggest nothing of their loss of racial vigor. They are the Henan boxers, the Shantung bandits and the imperial brigands who have furnished China with all the native imperial dynasties, the raw material from which the characters of Chinese novels of wars and adventure are drawn.

Down the south-east coast, south of the Yangtse, one meets a different type, inured to ease and culture and sophistication, mentally developed but physically retrograde, loving their poetry and their comforts, sleek undergrown men and slim neurasthenic women, fed on birds'-nest soup and lotus seeds, shrewd in business, gifted in belles-lettres, and cowardly in war, ready to roll on the ground and cry for

---

1. Lin, Yutang, *My Country and My People*, Beijing: Foreign Language Teaching and Research Publication, 2009.

mamma before the lifted fist descends, off-springs of the cultured Chinese families who crossed the Yangtse with their books and paintings during the end of the Ch'in Dynasty, when China was overrun by barbaric invaders.

South in Guangdong, one meets again a different people, where racial vigor is again in evidence, where people eat like men and work like men, enterprising, carefree, spendthrift, pugnacious, adventurous, progressive and quick-tempered, where beneath the Chinese culture a snake-eating aborigines tradition persists, revealing a strong admixture of the blood of the ancient Yue inhabitants of southern China, North and south of Hankou, in the middle of China, the loudswearing and intrigue-loving Hubei people exist, who are compared by the people of other provinces to "nine-headed birds in heaven" because they never say die, and who think pepper not hot enough to eat until they have fried it in oil, while the Hunan people, noted for their soldiery and their dogged persistence, offer a pleasanter variety of these descendants of the ancient Chu warriors.

Movements of trade and the imperial rule of sending scholars to official posts outside their native provinces l have brought about some mixture of the peoples and have smoothed out these provincial differences, but as a whole they continue to exist. For the significant fact remains that the northerner is essentially a conqueror and the southerner is essentially a trader, and that of all the imperial brigands who have founded Chinese dynasties, none have come from south of the Yangtse. The tradition developed that no rice-eating southerners could mount the dragon throne, and only noodle-eating northerners could. In fact, with the exception of the founders of the Tang and Zhou Dynasties, who emerged from north-east Gansu and were therefore Turkish-suspect, all the founders of the great dynasties have come from a rather restricted mountainous area, somewhere around the Longhai Railway, which includes eastern Henan, southern Hebei, western Shantung and northern Anhui. It should not be difficult to determine the mileage of the radius within which imperial babies were born with a point on the Longhai Railway as the center of the area. The founder of the Han Dynasty came from Peixian in modern Xuzhou that of the Qin Dynasty came from Henan, that of the Song Dynasty came from Gouxian in southern Hebei, and Zhu Hongwu of the Ming Dynasty came from Fengyang in Henan.

. . .

The raw, rugged North and the soft, pliable South—one can see these differences in their language, music and poetry. Observe the contrast between the Shaanxi songs, on the one hand, sung to the metallic rhythm of hard wooden tablets and keyed to a high pitch like the Swiss mountain songs, suggestive of the howling winds on mountain tops and broad pastures and desert sand-dunes, and on the other, the indolent Suzhou crooning, something that is between a sigh and a snore, throaty, nasal, and highly suggestive of a worn-out patient of asthma whose sighs and groans have by force of habit become swaying and rhythmic. In language, one sees the difference between the sonorous, clear-cut rhythm of Pekingese mandarin that pleases by its alternate light and shade, and the soft and sweet babbling of Suzhou women, with round-lip vowels and circumflex tones, where force of emphasis is not expressed by a greater explosion but by longdrawn-out and finely nuanced syllables at the end of sentences.

The story is recounted of a northern colonel who, on reviewing a Suzhou company, could not make the soldiers move by his explosive "Forward March!" The captain who had stayed a long time in Suzhou and who understood the situation asked permission to give the command in his own way. The permission was granted. Instead of the usual clear-cut "Kaibu Zou!" he gave a genuine persuasive Suzhou "kebu tser nyiaaaaaaaah!" and lo and behold! The Suzhou company moved.

Extensive Reading D

The History of China from 220 AD–1200 AD[1]

Herbert Allen Giles

The long-lived and glorious House of Han was brought to a close by the usual causes. There were palace intrigues and a temporary usurpation of the throne, eunuchs of course being in the thick of the mischief; added to which a very serious rebellion broke out, almost as a natural consequence. First and last there arose three aspirants to the Imperial yellow, which takes the place of purple in ancient Rome; the result being that, after some years of hard fighting, China was divided into three parts, each ruled by one of the three rivals. The period is known in history as that of the Three Kingdoms, and lasted from 220 AD to 265 AD. This short space of time was filled, especially the early years, with stirring deeds of heroism and marvelous strategical operations, fortune favoring first one of the three commanders and then another. The whole story of these civil wars is most graphically told in a famous historical romance composed about a thousand years afterwards. As in the case of the Waverley novels, a considerable amount of fiction has been interwoven with truth to make the narrative more palatable to the general reader; but its basis is history, and the work is universally regarded among the Chinese themselves as one of the most valuable productions in the lighter branches of their literature.

The three to four centuries which follow on the above period were a time of political and social disorganization, unfavorable, according to Chinese writers, to the development of both literature and art. The House of Chin, which at first held sway over a once more united empire, was severely harassed by the Tartars on the north, who were in turn overwhelmed by the House of Tuoba. The latter ruled for some two hundred years over northern China, while the southern portions were governed by several short-lived native dynasties. A few points in connection with these times deserve perhaps brief mention.

The old rule of twenty-seven months of mourning for parents was re-established, and has continued in force down to the present day. The Japanese sent occasional missions, with tribute; and the Chinese, who had already in 240

---

1. Herbert Allen Giles, *The Civilization of China*, Ibook.

AD dispatched an envoy to Japan, repeated the compliment in 608. An attempt was made to conquer Korea, and envoys were sent to countries as far off as Siam. Buddhism, which had been introduced many centuries previously—no one can exactly say when—began to spread far and wide, and appeared to be firmly established. In 399 AD a Buddhist priest, named Fa Xian, started from Central China and traveled to India across the great desert and over the Hindu Kush, subsequently visiting Patna, Benares, Buddha-Gaya, and other well-known spots, which he accurately described in the record of his journey published on his return and still in existence. His object was to obtain copies of the sacred books, relics and images, illustrative of the faith; and these he safely conveyed to China by sea from India, via Ceylon (where he spent three years), and Sumatra, arriving after an absence of fifteen years.

In the year 618 AD the House of Tang entered upon its glorious course of three centuries in duration. Under a strong but dissolute ruler immediately preceding, China had once more become a united empire, undivided against itself; and although wars and rebellions were not wanting to disturb the even tenor of its way, the general picture presented to us under the new dynasty of the Tangs is one of national peace, prosperity, and progress. The name of this House has endured, like that of Han, to the present day in the popular language of the people; for just as the northerners still delight to style themselves "good sons of Han," so are the southerners still proud to speak of themselves as "men of Tang."

One of the chief political events of this period was the usurpation of power by the Empress Wu—at first, as nominal regent on behalf of a step-child, the son and heir of her late husband by his first wife, and afterwards, when she had set aside the step-child, on her own account. There had been one previous instance of a woman wielding the Imperial scepter, namely, the Empress Lü of the Han dynasty, to whom the Chinese have accorded the title of legitimate ruler, which has not been allowed to the Empress Wu. The latter, however, was possessed of much actual ability, mixed with a kind of midsummer madness; and so long as her great intellectual faculties remained unimpaired, she ruled, like her successor of some twelve centuries afterwards, with a rod of iron. In her old age she was deposed and dismissed to private life, the rightful heir being replaced upon his father's throne.

. . .

Another striking picture of the Tang dynasty is presented by the career of an emperor who is usually spoken of as Ming Huang, and who, after distinguishing himself at several critical junctures, mounted the throne in 712 AD, in succession to his father, who had abdicated in his favor. He began with economy, closing the silk factories and forbidding the palace ladies to wear jewels or embroideries, considerable quantities of which were actually burnt. He was a warm patron of literature, and schools were established in every village. Fond of music, he founded a college for training youth of both sexes in this art. His love of war and his growing extravagance led to increased taxation, with the usual consequences in China—discontent and rebellion. He surrounded himself by a brilliant court, welcoming men of genius in literature and art; at first for their talents alone, but finally for their readiness to participate in scenes of revelry and dissipation provided for the amusement of a favorite concubine, the ever-famous Yang Gui Fei. Eunuchs were appointed to official posts, and the grossest forms of religious superstition were encouraged. Women ceased to veil themselves, as of old. At length, in 755 AD, a serious rebellion broke out, and a year later the emperor, now an old man of seventy-one, fled before the storm. He had not proceeded far before his soldiery revolted and demanded vengeance upon the whole family of the favorite, several unworthy members of which had been raised to high positions and loaded with honors. The wretched emperor was forced to order the head eunuch to strangle his idolized concubine, while the rest of her family perished at the hands of the troops. He subsequently abdicated in favor of his son, and spent the last six years of his life in seclusion.

. . .

The magnificent House of Tang was succeeded by five insignificant dynasties, the duration of all of which was crowded into about half a century. Then, in 960 AD, began the rule of the Songs, to last for three hundred years and rival in national peace and prosperity any other period in the history of China. The nation had already in a great measure settled down to that state of material civilization and mental culture in which it has remained to the present time. To the appliances of ordinary Chinese life it is probable that but few additions have been made since a very early date. The dress of the people has indeed undergone several variations, but the ploughs and hoes, the water-wheels and well-sweeps, the tools of the artisans, mud huts, carts, junks, chairs, tables, chopsticks, etc., which we still see in China, are probably very much those of two thousand years ago.

In spite, however, of the peaceful aspirations of the House of Song, the Khitan Tartars were forever encroaching upon Chinese territory, and finally overran and occupied a large part of northern China, with their capital where Peking now stands. This resulted in an amicable arrangement to divide the empire, the Khitans retaining their conquests in the north, from which, after about two hundred years, they were in turn expelled by the Golden Tartars, who had previously been subject to them.

Many volumes, rather than pages, would be required to do justice to the statesmen, soldiers, philosophers, poets, historians, art critics, and other famous men of this dynasty. It has already been stated that the interpretation of the

Confucian Canon, accepted at the present day, dates from this period; and it may now be of interest to give a brief account of another remarkable movement connected with the dynasty, though in quite a different line.

Wang Anshi, popularly known as the Reformer, was born in 1021 AD. In his youth a keen student, his pen seemed to fly over the paper. He rose to high office; and by the time he was fortyeight he found himself installed as confidential adviser to the emperor. He then entered upon a series of startling political reforms, said to be based upon new and more correct interpretations of portions of the Confucian Canon, which still remained, so far as explanation was concerned, just as it had been left by the scholars of the Han dynasty. This appeal to authority was, of course, a mere blind, cleverly introduced to satisfy the bulk of the population, who were always unwilling to move in any direction where no precedent is forthcoming. One of his schemes, the express object of which was to decrease taxation and at the same time to increase the revenue, was to secure a sure and certain market for all products, as follows. From the produce of a given district, enough was to be set aside (1) for the payment of taxes, and (2) to supply the wants of the district; (3) the balance was then to be taken over by the state at a low rate, and held for a rise or forwarded to some center where there happened to be a demand. There would be thus a certainty of market for the farmer, and an equal certainty for the state to make profits as a middleman. Another part of this scheme consisted in obligatory advances by the state to cultivators of land, whether these farmers required the money or not, the security for the loans being in each case the growing crops.

There was also a system of tithing for military purposes, under which every family having more than two males was bound to supply one to serve as a soldier; and in order to keep up a breed of cavalry horses, every family was compelled to take charge of one, which was provided, together with its food, by the government. There was a system under which money payments were substituted for the old-fashioned and vexatious method of carrying on public works by drafts of forced laborers; and again another under which warehouses for bartering and hypothecating goods were established all over the empire.

Of all his innovations the most interesting was that all land was to be remeasured and an attempt made to secure a more equitable incidence of taxation. The plan was to divide up the land into equal squares, and to levy taxes in proportion to the fertility of each. This scheme proved for various reasons to be unworkable; and the bitter opposition with which, like all his other measures of reform, it was received by his opponents, did not conduce to success. Finally, he abolished all restrictions upon the export of copper, the result being that even the current copper "cash" were melted down and made into articles for sale and exportation. A panic ensued, which Wang met by the simple expedient of doubling the value of each cash. He attempted to reform the examination system, requiring from the candidate not so much graces of style as a wide acquaintance with practical subjects. "Accordingly," says one Chinese author, "even the pupils at the village schools threw away their text-books of rhetoric, and began to study primers of history, geography, and political economy"—a striking anticipation of the movement in vogue today. "I have myself been," he tells us, "an omnivorous reader of books of all kinds, even, for example, of ancient medical and botanical works. I have, moreover, dipped into treatises on agriculture and on needlework, all of which I have found very profitable in aiding me to seize the great scheme of the Canon itself." But like many other great men, he was in advance of his age. He fell into disfavor at court, and was dismissed to a provincial post; and although he was soon recalled, he retired into private life, shortly afterwards to die, but not before he had seen the whole of his policy reversed.

Study Questions

1. What is the basic structure of the hexagrams in *I Ching* or *The Book of Changes*? What is the order to read each of the grams? Try to follow such an order and read the gram explanations in the selected text and tell what lessons are offered in Qian and Kun hexagrams?

2. How would you consider your present phase of life placed in the hexagram of Qian or Kun?

3. Legend has it that King Wen made decisions on the hexagrams of *I Ching* when imprisoned by King Zhou of Shang Dynasty, King Wu prepared and seized the best moment for throwing over the ruling of Shang, and King Cheng established a solid sovereignty of Zhou with the help majorly from the Duke of Zhou. Can you illustrate the whole process of the founding of the new kingdom using the philosophical concepts revealed from the hexagrams of Qian and Kun?

4. Explain the reasons for and comment on the careful planning and organization of the capital moving by the Duke of Zhou and the Duke of Shao.

5. Are you from the North or the South of China? Do you agree with what Lin Yutang has elaborated on the differences between people from different areas of the country? How has the idea of the "central plain" changed throughout history until today?

6. Please use the philosophical ideas you have learned from *I Ching* to explain the excerpted description of Chinese history in Herbert Allen Giles's text.

7. Read Giles's narrative of the Reformation by Wang Anshi, and figure out why Wang Anshi claimed that the reforms were based on a more correct interpretation of the Confucius Canon?

8. Giovan Battista Vico, the Italian political philosopher, wrote in his magnum opus, *New Science* that:

   "He (Sanchuniathon) wrote the history of Phoenicia in vulgar characters, while the Egyptians and the Scythians, as we have seen, wrote in hieroglyphs, as the Chinese have been found to do down to our own days. The latter, like the Scythians and the Egyptians, boasted a monstrous antiquity because in the darkness of their isolation, having no dealings with other nations, they had no true idea of time"; "Idanthyrsus must have been like one of the Chinese kings who, up to a few centuries ago cut off from the rest of the world, vainly boast an antiquity greater than that of the world, and, after so long a time, are still found writing with hieroglyphs, and, although on account of the great mildness of the climate they have most refined talents and make so many marvelously delicate things, do not yet know how to make shadows in painting, against which highlights can stand out; whence, since it has neither relief nor depth, their painting is most crude. And as for the statuettes of porcelain which come from there, they show the Chinese to be just as unskilled as the Egyptians were in casting; whence it may be inferred that the Egyptians were as unskilled in painting as the Chinese are now."[1]

Focus on Vico's comment on China that impressed him, and ask yourself whether he was being fair enough in his judgments. Which points do you not agree with? Do some research on those points and make a counterargument against Vico.

---

1. Thomas Goddard Bergin and Max Harold Fisch (trans.), *New Science of Giambattista Vico*, New York: Cornell University Press, 1948.

CHAPTER ❷

The Development of Confucianism

Pre-reading Questions

1. In *The Records of the Grand Historian*, Sima Qian listed Confucius in the section of "Hereditary Houses" and gave us the earliest biographical sketch of "Confucius the Man" instead of "Confucius the Saint." Try to understand Confucius and the other important Confucians through the readings in this Chapter as gently men and tell what temperament and personalities they have?

2. If you compare the images on ancient Greek artifacts excavated that suggest the ritual happenings and those on ancient Chinese ritual vessels, you may figure that there are sharp differences between them. Among other things, you would see images of actual individuals practicing a ritual on a red-figure ancient Greek vase which is replaced by totemic symbols on a Chinese counter-part. How do you explain such a contrast?

3. Interview a friend from another country or culture and ask whether he knows something about "Li" or "Ren" in Confucianism.

Introduction

The key to understanding Confucius's ideas is the Confucian nostalgia of falling back on the glorious tribal society where the leaders were models of virtue and the commoners practiced propriety. These became treasures to exist mostly with idealists who lived in a time when court intrigues, military frictions and political turmoil found their way into the later years of Western Zhou Dynasty. With a sense of disappointment at the present, Confucius envisioned a future with a view to the past and believed to resume the principles of rites and propriety of the "Golden Age" might be a remedy.

Confucius attached "Li" with ideals more than what rites and propriety could ever contain, hence making the Chinese word "Li" one of those cultural concepts that has yielded unlimited versions of translation and explanation. From the formation of this ideograph, the character has its ceremonial origin, with its radical on the left referring to paying tribute in rituals, on the right two pieces of jade as sacrificial articles and an ancient drum played on the scene. Though Confucius is said to be an expert in ritual formality, being a lover for ceremonial games since when he was little, this stress on the formality of rituals never outranks one's sincerity in his respects and compassion of those who deserve, according to a Confucian ethical principle, to be respected and sympathized at rituals or ceremonies.

What constitutes the ethical principle is what distinguishes Confucianism from the other schools of Chinese thoughts. We often use "Ren" to explain such a unique principle. When examined from the structural build-up of the Chinese character, Ren, it exposes itself as a combination of yang and yin principles, with the left part referring to the solid line of yang standing up, and the right part the broken line of yin parted up and down. This relates us back to the Confucian classic of *I Ching*, and its encapsulating wisdom of the dynamic movement between yin and yang principles. Yet what is fore-grounded in Confucianism is the order and interactivity between the two principles with yang being the initiative one, hence we see a strong sense of hierarchy in Confucianism. With the leading role of the "yang," as embodied in older brothers, fathers, rulers, and kings, the embodiment of yin, younger brothers, women, the subordinate, and the officials were supposed to carry the ideally designed virtues of the yin principle and follow the initiative roles, thus creating the structural and cultural harmony of the hierarchy. What needs to be clarified is that the connection between Confucianism and the working of yin and yang had not been conspicuously laid out until being elaborated in Neo-Confucian classics during Song dynasty, the school of which was started with the significant impact of Zhou Dunyi, the important scholar and philosopher of the Song Dynasty.

One theory that argues for the validity of the Confucian ethical principle is what is termed as "compassion extension," in which the love of oneself and one's own blood kindred should and can be extended to other relations without disruption. Mencius, the "Second Confucian Sage" emphasized the yin side of such a "compassion extension" in his "Li Lou" Chapter, where he described a huge power produced by a sagely person of forbearance and forgiveness over the ungentle and immoral. And with an implicit logic of "compassion extension," he suggested that the source of such a great power to tolerate others could be found in one's unbounded love to one's own offspring. Xunzi, on the other hand, highlighted the yang side of the "compassion extension," emphasizing one's self-motivation and cultivation to achieve the status of a Confucian gentleman. The spiritual forbearance was thus less sensed in Xunzi's vital-energyridden prose, while behavioral training and habit-forming geared toward a Confucian superior man were thoroughly argued and evidenced. In the Chapter of "The Merit of the Confucian," the "compassion extension" mechanism was used in his quotation of lines from *The Book of Odes* or *Classic of Poetry*, where the rulers were admonished by the fear that once a hard-hearted man was favored and promoted, the dissatisfaction against this single event might be extended to a more general mistrust of the governance.

Selected Passages from *The Analects*[1]

《论语》选篇

Political Ideas: "Ren" and Propriety

2.3 Confucius said: "Lead the people by laws and regulate them by penalties, and the people will try to keep out of jail, but will have no sense of shame. Lead the people by virtue and restrain them by the rules of decorum, and the people will have a sense of shame, and moreover will become good."

3.4 Lin Fang asked what was the first thing to be attended to in ceremonies. The Master said, "A great question indeed! In festive ceremonies, it is better to be sparing than extravagant. In the ceremonies of mourning, it is better that there be deep sorrow than in minute attention to observances."

3.19 The Duke Ding asked how a prince should employ his ministers, and how ministers should serve their prince. Confucius replied, "A prince should employ his minister according to the rules of propriety; ministers should serve their prince with faithfulness."

12.17 Ji Kangzi asked Confucius about government. Confucius said: "To govern is to set things right. If you begin by setting yourself right, who will dare deviate from the right."

12.19 Ji Kangzi asked Confucius about government, saying: "Suppose I were to kill the lawless for the good of the law-abiding, how would that do?" Confucius answered: "Sir, why should it be necessary to employ capital punishment in your government? Just so you genuinely desire the good, the people will be good. The virtue of the gentleman may be compared to the wind and that of the commoner to the weeds. The weeds under the force of the wind cannot but bend."

2.3 子曰: "道之以政, 齐之以刑, 民免而无耻; 道之以德, 齐之以礼, 有耻且格。"

3.4 林放问礼之本。子曰: "大哉问! 礼, 与其奢也, 宁俭; 丧, 与其易也, 宁戚。"

3.19 定公问: "君使臣, 臣事君, 如之何?" 孔子对曰: "君使臣以礼, 臣事君以忠。"

12.17 季康子问政于孔子。孔子对曰: "政者, 正也。子帅以正, 孰敢不正?"

12.19 季康子问政于孔子曰: "如杀无道, 以就有道, 何如?" 孔子对曰: "子为政, 焉用杀? 子欲善, 而民善矣。君子之德风, 小人之德草。草上之风, 必偃。"

---

1. WM. Theodore De Bary, Wing-Tsit Chan, and Burton Watson, *Sources of Chinese Tradition*, New York: Columbia University Press, 1960.

Ethical Ideas: "Ren" and Benevolence

4.15 The Master said, "Shen, my doctrine is that of an allpervading unity." The disciple Zeng replied, "Yes." The Master went out, and the other disciples asked, saying, "What do his words mean?" Zeng said, "The doctrine of our master is to be true to the principles of our nature and the benevolent exercise of them to others (reciprocity), —this and nothing more."

8.2 Confucius said: "Courtesy without decorum becomes tiresome. Cautiousness without decorum becomes timidity, daring becomes offensiveness, frankness becomes effrontery."

12.3 Sima Niu asked about perfect virtue. The Master said, "The man of perfect virtue is cautious and slow in his speech." "Cautious and slow in his speech!" said Niu: "Is this what is meant by perfect virtue?" The Master said, "When a man feels the difficulty of doing, can he be other than cautious and slow in speaking?"

15.24 Zi Gong asked, "Is there one word which may serve as a rule of practice for all one's life?" The Master said, "Is not RECIPROCITY such a word? What you do not want done to yourself, do not do to others."

4.15 子曰："参乎！吾道一以贯之。"曾子曰："唯。"子出。门人问曰："何谓也？"曾子曰："夫子之道，忠恕而已矣。"

8.2 子曰："恭而无礼则劳，慎而无礼则葸，勇而无礼则乱，直而无礼则绞。"

12.3 司马牛问仁。子曰："仁者其言也讱。"曰："其言也讱，斯谓之仁已乎？"子曰："为之难，言之得无讱乎？"

15.24 子贡问曰："有一言而可以终身行之者乎？"子曰："其恕乎！己所不欲，勿施于人。"

Selected Passages from *Mencius* [1]

由是观之,无恻隐之
心，非人也；无羞恶之
心，非人也；无辞让之
心，非人也；无是非之
心，非人也。恻隐之心，
仁之端也；羞恶之心义
之端也；辞让之心，礼
之端也；是非之心，智
之端也。人之有是四端
也，犹其有四体也。

From this case we may perceive that he who lacks the feeling of commiseration is not a man; that he who lacks a feeling of shame and dislike is not a man; that he who lacks a feeling of modesty and yielding is not a man; that he who lacks a sense of right and wrong is not a man. The feeling of commiseration is the beginning of human-heartedness. The feeling of shame and dislike is the beginning of righteousness. The feeling of modesty and yielding is the beginning of propriety. The sense of right and wrong is the beginning of wisdom. Man has these four beginnings, just as he has four limbs.

"What is the vast vital energy?"

"敢问何谓浩然之
气？"

"It is difficult to make it clear. Such vital energy is most great and indomitable. If it is nourished with integrity without our doing anything detrimental to it, it will be omnipresent, filling the whole universe. And it must be integrated with righteousness and morality, otherwise it becomes impotent.

曰："难言也。其
为气也，至大至刚；以
直养而无害，则塞于天
地之间。其为气也，配
义与道；无是，馁矣。

Such vital energy results from steady accumulation of righteousness and cannot be acquired through occasional righteous acts. If you have something on your conscience, it will become impotent."

是集义所生者，非
义袭而取之也。行有不
慊于心，则馁矣。"

Mencius said, "A gentleman differs from the ordinary run of people in that he preserves his heart. He preserves his heart through benevolence and decorum. A man of benevolence loves others; a man of decorum respects others. One who loves others is always loved by others; one who respects others is always respected by others. Suppose someone is impudent to him, he will examine and criticize himself, saying, 'It must be owing to the fact that I am not benevolent or decorous enough to him that he should treat me so.' When upon self-examination he finds himself

孟子曰："君子所
以异于人者，以其存心
也。君子以仁存心，以
礼存心。仁者爱人，有
礼者敬人。爱人者，人
恒爱之；敬人者，人恒
敬之。有人于此，其待
我以横逆则君子必自反
也：我必不仁也，必无
礼也；此物奚宜至哉！
其自反而仁矣，自反而

1. Yang Bojun, et al, *Mencius*, Changsha: Hunan People's Publishing House, 2009.

genuinely benevolent and decorous, and yet the other person continues to be impudent, he will examine and criticize himself again, saying, 'I must have been disloyal to him.' When upon a second self-examination, he finds nothing amiss with his loyalty, and the other person continues to be impudent, he will say, 'This fellow is indeed out of his head. He is no different from a beast. Why should I find fault with a beast?' Thus a gentleman may have lingering worries, but no sudden pains. He may be worried like this: Shun was a man, I am also one. Shun is the model of all the world, his name will ever inspire posterity to nobility, while I am quite ordinary. This is my only worry.

How should I strive to relieve myself of this worry? The best way is to learn from Shun. A gentleman has nothing else to worry about. He will do nothing that is not benevolent, nor will he violate the rites. When a gentleman is hit by a disaster that comes out of the blue, his heart still remains the seat of serenity.

As for a man, he should live in the spacious mansion of the world (benevolence), occupy the most proper position of the world (decorum), and walk down the broadest way of the world (righteousness). If he achieves his aim, he will go along the way together with the people; if he fails to achieve his aim, he will adhere to his own principles. He cannot be led into dissipation by wealth and rank, nor deflected from his aim by poverty and obscurity, nor made to bend by power and force—all this is characteristic of a great man."

有礼矣，其横逆由是也；君子必自反也：我必不忠。自反而忠矣，其横逆由是也。君子曰：'此亦妄人也已矣！如此则与禽兽奚择哉！于禽兽又何难焉！'是故，君子有终身之忧，无一朝之患也。乃若所忧则有之。舜，人也，我亦人也；舜为法于天下可传于后世，我由未免为乡人也：是则可忧也。

忧之如何？如舜而已矣！若夫君子所患，则亡矣。非仁无为也，非礼无行也。如有一朝之患。则君子不患矣。

居天下之广居，立天下之正位，行天下之大道；得志与民由之；不得志，独行其道。富贵不能淫，贫贱不能移，威武不能屈。此之谓大丈夫。"

"The Merit of the Confucian" from *The Works of Xunzi*[1]

A visitor said: "Confucius said, 'was Duke Zhou very virtuous? When he took high position[2], he was all the more respectful of others; when he became rich he was all the more stingy; when he had conquered his enemies he was all the more prepared for war.'"

In reply I said: "This is impertinent. It was not the conduct of Duke Zhou and not the saying of Confucius. When King Wu died, King Cheng was a minor; Duke Zhou protected King Cheng and succeeded to King Wu; he took the throne of the Emperor. When he turned his back to the screen[3] and arose, the feudal nobles hastened to go below the hall[4]. At such a time who was respectful of others!"

"He ruled the whole country and established seventy-one feudal states; of the Ji family there were enfeoffed fifty-three. If a descendant of the Zhou dynasty was not mad or deluded he certainly was made one of the glorious feudal nobles of the empire; who would say that Duke Zhou was stingy!"

"When King Wu put Zhou[5] to death, he did it on a day that the soldiers dreaded[6]; he faced east and resisted the great year[7]; then he got to the Fan, it was overflowing; when he got to Huai, the road was impassable; when he

《荀子·儒效》选篇

客有道曰：孔子曰："周公其盛乎！身贵而愈恭，家富而愈俭，胜敌而愈戒。"

应之曰：是殆非周公之行，非孔子之言也。武王崩，成王幼，周公屏成王而及武王，履天子之籍，负扆而立，诸侯趋走堂下。当是时也，夫又谁为恭矣哉！

兼制天下立七十一国，姬姓独居五十三人焉；周之子孙，苟不狂惑者，莫不为天下之显诸侯。孰谓周公俭哉！

武王之诛纣也，行之日以兵忌，东面而迎太岁，至泛而泛，至怀而坏，至共头而山隧。霍叔惧曰："出三日而五灾至，无乃不可乎？"

1. Homer H. Dubs (trans.), *The Works of Hsuntzu*, London: Arthur Probsthain, 1928.
2. became Regent
3. The silken screen in the audience chamber between the door and window. It was ornamented with hatches and axeheads.
4. Audience ended.
5. The tyranny Zhou of Shang Dynasty, Zhouxin (纣辛).
6. On the Jia Zi day, superstitiously avoided, King Wu joined battle with Zhou Xin's forces.
7. When King Wu was pursuing Zhou, Yu Xin advised him not to go northward because the planet Jupiter was in the north; but King Wu did not heed this superstitious advice. Jupiter is called the Sui Xing because twelve of its courses through the zodiac make the great year Tai Sui.

got to Gongtou, the mountain fell. Huoshu[1] was afraid, and said: "Is it not then quite probable that within three days the five calamities will visit us?"

"Duke Zhou said, 'He disemboweled Bigan, and imprisoned the viscount of Ji[2]; Feilian and Wulai[3] rule the government; why is anything probable?' Follow with the horse in ordered ranks and go forward! In the morning they ate at Qi; in the evening they lodged at the Hundred Springs; at dawn they settled at the Wilderness of Mu. They beat their drums and Zhou's troops easily submitted; thereupon they overthrew the people of Yin and killed Zhou. Then those who did the killing were not the people of Zhou but because of the people of Yin. Hence there were no taking of heads or captives, no rewards for difficult feats. On the contrary, they hung up the three kinds of defensive armor and put down the five kinds of weapons; they united the country and established their music; thereupon the Wu and Xiang[4] arose and the Shao and Hu[5] ceased. No one within the four seas failed to change his feelings and alter his reflections to be moved by them and obey them. Hence people did not close their outside doors; in crossing the country there were no boundaries[6]; in such a situation who would be prepared for war?"

Zaofu was the best charioteer in the world, but without a chariot and horses his ability could not have been seen. Yi was the best archer in the world, but without a bow and arrows his skill could not have been seen. The great Confucian is the best harmonizer and unifier in the world, but without a place of a hundred li, his merit cannot be seen.

If the chariot is good and the horses select, and yet a man cannot hereby travel far, a thousand li in one day, then he is not a Zaofu. If the bow is adjusted and the

周公曰："刳比干
而囚箕子，飞廉、恶
来知政，夫又恶有不可
焉！"
遂选马而进，朝食于
戚，暮宿于百泉，旦厌
于牧之野。鼓之而纣卒
易乡，遂乘殷人而诛
纣。盖杀者非周人，因
殷人也。故无首虏之
获，无蹈难之赏。反而
定三革，偃五兵，合天
下，立声乐，于是武象
起而韶护废矣。四海之
内，莫不变心易虑以化
顺之。故外阖不闭，
跨天下而无蕲。当是
时也，夫又谁为戒矣
哉！"

造父者，天下之善
御者也，无舆马则无所
见其能。羿者，天下之
善射者也，无弓矢则无
所见其巧。大儒者，善
调一天下者也，无百里
之地则无所见其功。

舆固马选矣，而不
能以至远，一日而千
里，则非造父也。弓调

---

1. The eighth son of King Wen, a younger brother of Duke Zhou.
2. A relative who remonstrated with Zhou Xin.
3. Two "favorites," one a good runner and the other a strong man.
4. Both are music of the Zhou Dynasty.
5. Both are music of the Yin Dynasty. The Shao was Shun's music.
6. It was like one family.

arrow is straight, and yet thereby a man cannot send it far and hit the bulls' eye, then he is not a Yi. If a man controls a place of a hundred li, but yet cannot harmonize and unify the whole country, and rule the strong and oppressive, then he is not a great Confucian.

. . . .

If a man is without a teacher or precepts, he will exalt his original nature[1]; if he has a teacher and precepts, he will exalt self-cultivation. Now a teacher and precepts are what is gained by self-cultivation, not what is obtained from original nature. Original nature is not good enough to set itself up as the ruler of a personality.

Original nature is that which I cannot produce, yet which can be developed. Self-cultivation is that which I do not originally have, but which can be produced. Choices and rejections and habitual practice are the means of developing original nature. To concentrate on one thing and not vary is that whereby selfcultivation is perfected.

Practice alters a person's inclinations; if kept up for a long time it alters his inmost being. If a person concentrates on one thing, and does not vary, he will become as wise as the gods and form a triad with Heaven and Earth. For by collecting earth a mountain is made, and by collecting water the sea is made. ... If the common man on the street cultivates goodness and wholly completes its cultivation, he will be called a Sage. First he must seek, and then only will he obtain; he must do it, and then only will he reach perfection; he must cultivate it, and then only can he rise; he must complete its cultivation, and then only can he be a Sage. For the Sage is the man who has cultivated himself. A man who practices hoeing and plowing becomes a farmer; if he practices chopping and shaving wood, he becomes an artisan; if he practices trafficking in goods, he becomes a merchant; if he practices the rules of proper conduct (Li) and justice (Yi), he becomes a superior *man*. ... The son of an artisan always follows his father's trade, and the people

矢直矣，而不能射远中微，则非羿也。用百里之地，而不能以调一天下，制强暴，则非大儒也。

……

人无师法，则隆性矣；有师法，则隆积矣。而师法者，所得乎积，非所受乎性。性不足以独立而治。性者也，吾所不能为也，然而可化也。积也者，非吾所有也，然而可为也。

注错习俗，所以化性也；并一而不二，所以成积也。

习俗移志，安久移质。并一而不二，则通于神明，参于天地矣。故积土而为山，积水而为海。…… 涂之人百姓，积善而全尽，谓之圣人。彼求之而后得，为之而后成，积之而后高，尽之而后圣，故圣人也者，人之所积也。人积耨耕而为农夫，积斲削而为工匠，积反货而为商贾，积礼义而为君子。……

---

1. Which is evil, and so the man will be led into evil.

of a city or state are satisfied to repeat its peculiarities. He who lives in Chu becomes a man of Chu; he who lives in Yue becomes a man of Yue; he who lives in central China becomes a man of central China. This is not from the original human nature received from Nature, but attained by profuse cultivation. Hence, if a man knows how to pay attention to his choices and rejections, to be careful of his habits, and to magnify profuse cultivation, he will become a superior man. If he follows his nature and his emotions, and his scholarship is restricted, he will become a small-minded man. If a person is a superior man he is usually peaceful and honored; if he is a small-minded man he is usually in danger and disgrace. All men desire peace and honor and dislike danger and disgrace; hence the superior man alone is able to obtain that which he likes; the small-minded man daily invites that which he dislikes. The ode[1] says:

故人知谨注错，慎习俗，大积靡，则为君子矣。纵情性而不足问学，则为小人矣；为君子则常安荣矣，为小人则常危辱矣。

凡人莫不欲安荣而恶危辱，故唯君子为能得其所好，小人则日徼其所恶。诗曰：

    "Now this good man
Is not sought after nor
advances in office.
But that hard-hearted man
Is thought of and promoted
again and again.
So the people are avaricious
and disorderly
And prefer ways which are
like poisonous weeds."
—this expresses my meaning.

    "维此良人，
弗求弗迪；

唯彼忍心，
是顾是复。

民之贪乱，

宁为荼毒。"

此之谓也。

---

1. *Book of Odes*, III, iii, 11. A lament over the misgovernment of King Li (878–842 BC)—he advanced the evil and neglected the worthy, hence the people were led into evil. Such is the action of the small minded man when in control of the State.

An Explanation of the Diagram of the Great Ultimate

太极图说

Zhou Dunyi[1]

周敦颐

The Non-ultimate! And also the Great Ultimate. The Great Ultimate through movement generates the yang. When its activity reaches its limit, it becomes tranquil. Through tranquility the Great Ultimate generates the yin. When tranquility reaches its limit, activity begins again. Thus movement and tranquility alternate and become the root of each other, giving rise to the distinction of yin and yang, and these two modes are thus established.

无极而太极。太极动而 生阳, 动极而静; 静而生阴, 静极复动。一动一静, 互为 其根; 分阴分阳, 两仪立焉。

By the transformation of yang and its union with yin, the five agents of water, fire, wood, metal, and earth arise. When these five material-forces (qi[2]) are distributed in harmonious order, the four seasons run their course.

阳变阴合而生水火木金 土, 五气顺布, 四时运焉。

The five agents constitute one system of yin and yang, and yin and yang constitute one Great Ultimate. The Great Ultimate is fundamentally the Non-ultimate. The five agents arise, each with its specific nature.

五行一阴阳也, 阴阳一太极也, 太极本无极也。五行之生也, 各一其性。

When the reality of the Non-ultimate and the essence of yin and yang and the five agents come into mysterious union, integration ensues. The heavenly principle (qian) constitutes the male element, and the earthly principle (kun) constitutes the female element. The interaction of these two material forces engenders and transforms the myriad things, the myriad things produce and reproduce, resulting in an unending transformation.

无极之真, 二五之精, 妙合而凝。乾道成男, 坤道成女。二气交感, 化生万物, 万物生生而变化无穷焉。

It is man alone who receives [the material force] in their highest excellence, and therefore he is most

唯人也得其秀而为灵。形既生矣, 神发知矣, 五性感动而善恶分, 万事出矣。

---

1. WM. Theodore de Bary, Wing-Tsit Chan, and Burton Watson, *Sources of Chinese Tradition*, New York: Columbia University Press, 1960: p. 458.
2. Rendered "vital force(s)" as it appears in earlier sources, qi is modified to "material force" in this chapter where its role as the basic matter or stuff of the universe is stressed. Other widely used translation for qi are "ether" and "matter energy."

intelligent. His corporeal form appears, and his spirit develops consciousness. The five moral principles of his nature (humanity, righteousness, decorum, wisdom, and good faith) are aroused by, and react to, the external world and engage in activity; good and evil are distinguished and human affairs take place.

The sage orders these affairs by the principles of the Mean, correctness, humanity, and righteousness, considering tranquility to be the ruling factor. Thus he establishes himself as the ultimate standard for man. Hence the character of the sages is "identical with that of Heaven and earth; his brilliance is identical with that of the sun and moon; his order is identical with that of the four seasons; and his good and evil fortunes are identical with those of heavenly and earthly spirits."

圣人定之以中正仁义而主静，立人极焉。故圣人"与天地合其德，日月合其明，四时合其序，鬼神合其吉凶。"

The gentleman cultivates these moral qualities and enjoys good fortune, whereas the inferior man violates them and suffers evil fortune.

君子修之吉，小人悖之凶。

Therefore it is said: "The yin and yang are established as the way of heaven; the elements of strength and weakness as the way of earth; and humanity and righteousness as the way of man."[1] It is also said there: "If we investigate into the cycle of things, we shall understand the concepts of life and death."[2] Great is *The Book of Changes*! Herein lies its excellence!

故曰：立天之道曰阴与阳；立地之道曰柔与刚；立人之道曰仁与义。又曰，原始反终，故知死生之说。大哉易也，斯其至矣！

---

1. From *The Book of Changes (I Ching)*, Shuo Gua .
2. From *The Book of Changes (I Ching)*, Zhu Xi I.

Extensive Reading A

Chapter Nine from
The Book of Rites[1]

One day Confucius went to see the ceremony of Zha. After the ceremony was over, Confucius took a walk. He stopped at a roadhouse on the side of the city gate (overlooking the suburb) and heaved a deep sigh. Confucius was sighing over the social conditions in his state Lu. Yanyan was with him, and asked Confucius, "Why are you sighing?" And Confucius replied, "Oh, I was thinking of the Golden Age and regretting that I was not able to have been born in it and to be associated with the wise rulers and ministers of the Three Dynasties. How I would have loved to have lived in such an age!

When the great Dao prevailed (i.e. in the Golden Age), the world was a common state (not belonging to any particular ruling family), rulers were elected according to their wisdom and ability and mutual confidence and peace prevailed. Therefore people not only regarded their own parents as parents and their own children as children. The old people were able to enjoy their old age, the young men were able to employ their talent, the juniors had the elders to look up to, and the helpless widows, orphans and cripples and deformed were well taken care of. The men had their respective occupations and the women had their homes. If the people didn't want to see goods lying about on the ground, they did not have to keep them for themselves, and if people had too much energy for work, they did not have to labor for their own profit. Therefore there was no cunning or intrigue and there were no bandits or burglars, and as a result, there was no need to shut one's outer gate (at night). This was the period of

《礼记·礼运》
选篇

昔者仲尼与于蜡宾，事毕，出游于观之上，喟然而叹。仲尼之叹，盖叹鲁也。言偃在侧曰："君子何叹？"孔子曰："大道之行也，与三代之英，丘未之逮也，而有志焉。"

大道之行也，天下为公。选贤与能，讲信修睦，故人不独亲其亲，不独子其子，使老有所终，壮有所用，

幼有所长，矜寡孤独废疾者，皆有所养。男有分，女有归。货，恶其弃于地也，不必藏于己；力，恶其不出于身也，不必为己。

是故，谋闭而不兴，盗窃乱贼而不作，故外户而不闭，是谓大同。

---

1. Lin Yutang, *The Wisdom of Confucius*, Beijing: Qunyan Press, 2010.

Datong, or the Great Commonwealth.

But now the great Dao no longer prevails, and the world is divided up into private families (or becomes the possession of private families), and people regard only their own parents as parents and only their own children as children. They acquire goods and labor each for his own benefit. A hereditary aristocracy is established and the different states build cities, outer cities and moats each for its own defense. The principles of "Li" (or forms of social intercourse) and righteousness serve as the principles of social discipline. By means of these principles, people try to maintain the official status of rulers and subjects, to teach the parents and children and elder brothers and younger brothers and husbands and wives to live in harmony, to establish social institutions and to live in groups of hamlets. The physically strong and the mentally clever are raised to prominence and each other tries to carve his own career. Hence there is deceit and cunning and from these wars arise. (The great founders of dynasties like) Emperors Yu, Tang, Wen, Wu and Cheng and Duke Zhou were the best men of this age. Without a single exception, these six gentlemen were deeply concerned over the principle of "Li," through which justice was maintained, general confidence was tested, and errors or malpractices were exposed. An ideal of true manhood, "ren," was set up and good manners or courtesy was cultivated, as solid principles for the common people to follow. A ruler who violates these principles would then be denounced as a public enemy and driven off from his office. This is called the Period of Xiaokang, or The Period of Minor Peace.

...

In the ancient times, the rulers did not have houses, and they lived in dug-out caves or in piled-up mounds in winter and on "nests" made of dry branches (on top of trees) in summer. They did not know the use of fire, but ate fruits and the flesh of birds and animals, drinking their blood, including the hair in it. They did not have hemp cloth or silk and were clothed in feathers and animal skins.

今大道既隐，天下为家，各亲其亲，各子其子，货力为己，大人世及以为礼。城郭沟池以为固，礼义以为纪；

以正君臣，以笃父子，以睦兄弟，以和夫妇，以设制度，以立田里，以贤勇知，以功为己。

故谋用是作，而兵由此起。禹汤文武成王周公，由此其选也。此六君子者，未有不谨于礼者也。以著其义，以考其信，著有过，刑仁讲让，示民有常。如有不由此者，在执者去，众以为殃，是谓小康。"

......

昔者先王未有宫室，冬则居营窟，夏则居曾巢。未有火化，食草木之实，鸟兽之肉，饮其血，茹其毛。未有麻丝，衣其羽皮。后圣有作，然后修火之利，

Later came the Sages who taught them the use of fire, and they cast metalware by pouring it into bamboo molds and to mold clay into earthenware. Then they built terraces and houses with doors and windows, and began to bake and broil and cook and roast by means of a spit, and made wine and vinegar. They began also to use hemp and silk and weave them into cloth for the use of the living and sacrifices to the dead and the worship of the spirits and God. These ancient practices were also handed down from the early times. Therefore, the black wine was kept in the inner room, the white wine was kept near the (southern) door, the red wine was kept in the hall and the heavy wine was kept still further outside. The meat offerings were then displayed and the round tripod and the square vessel were laid in order, and the musical instruments, the qin, se, the flute, the ching (musical stone suspended from a string and struck like bells), the bell and the drum were arranged in their places, and the sacrificial prayer to the dead and the answer from the dead were carefully prepared and read, that the celestial and the ancestors' spirits might descend to the place of worship. All these practices were for the purpose of maintaining the proper status of rulers and subjects, maintaining the love between parents and children, teaching kindness between brothers, regulating relationships between superiors and inferiors, and establishing the respective relationships of husband and wife, to the end that all might be blessed by Heaven. They then prepared the sacrificial lamentations. The black or dark wine was used for sacrifice, and the blood and hair of the animals were used in offering, and the raw meat was placed in a square vessel. Burnt meat was also offered, a mat was spread out and a piece of coarse cloth was used for covering the vessels, and silk ceremonial robes were used. The different wines, Li and Qian, and baked and broiled meats were also offered. The sovereign and the queen made the offerings alternately, that the good spirits might descend and they might be united with the occult world. After the sacrifices were over, they then gave a feast to the guests, dividing up the dogs, pigs, cows and

范金合土，以为台榭宫室牖户，以炮以燔，以亨以炙，以为醴酪，治其麻丝，以为布帛，以养生送死，以事鬼神上帝，皆从其朔。

故玄酒在室，醴盏在户，粢醍在堂，澄酒在下。

陈其牺牲，备其鼎俎，列其琴瑟管磬钟鼓，修其祝嘏，以降上神与其先祖，以正君臣，

以笃父子，以睦兄弟，以齐上下，夫妇有所。是谓承天之祐。作其祝号，玄酒以祭，荐其血毛，腥其俎，孰其殽，与其越席，疏布以幂，衣其浣帛，醴盏以献，荐其燔炙，

君与夫人交献，以嘉魂是谓合莫。然后退而合亨，体其犬豕牛羊，实其簠簋笾豆铏羹。祝以孝告，嘏以慈告，是谓

lambs at the offering and placing them in various vessels.
The prayer to the dead declared the gratitude or loyalty
of the living, and the answer from the dead declared the
continued affection of the deceased. This was the great
blessing and accomplishment of "Li."

大祥，此礼之大成也。

Extensive Reading B

"The Great Harmony" from *Correcting Youthful Ignorance*

《正蒙·太和》选篇

Zhang Zai[1]

张载

The Great Harmony is called the Way (Dao, Moral Law). It embraces the nature which underlies all counter processes of floating and sinking, rising and falling, and motion and rest. It is the origin of the process of fusion and intermingling, of overcoming and being overcome, and of expansion and contraction. At the commencement, these processes are incipient, subtle, obscure, easy, and simple, but at the end they are extensive, great, strong, and firm. It is qian (Heaven) that begins with the knowledge of Change, and kun (Earth) that models after simplicity. That which is dispersed, differentiated, and capable of assuming form becomes material force (qi), and that which is pure, penetrating, and not capable of assuming form becomes spirit. Unless the whole universe is in the process of fusion and intermingling like fleeting forces moving in all directions, it may not be called Great Harmony. When those who talk about the Way know this, then they really know the Way, and when those who study Change (or *The Book of Changes*) understand this, then they really understand Change. Otherwise, even though they possess the admirable talents of Duke Zhou, their wisdom is not praiseworthy.

太和所谓道，中涵浮沈、升降、动静、相感之性，是生絪缊、相荡、胜负、屈伸之始。其来也几微易简，其究也广大坚固。起知于易者乾乎！效法于简者坤乎！散殊而可象为气，清通而不可象为神。不如野马、絪缊，不足谓之太和。

The Great Vacuity (Xu) has no physical form. It is the original substance of material force. Its integration and disintegration are but objectifications caused by Change. Human nature at its source is absolutely tranquil and unaffected by externality. When it is affected by contact

语道者知此，谓之知道；学易者见此，谓之见易。不如是，虽周公才美，其智不足称也已。

太虚无形，气之本体，其聚其散，变化之客形尔；至静无感，性之渊源，有识有知，物交之客感尔。客感客形与无感无形，惟尽性者一之。

1. Wing-Tsit Chan, *A Source Book in Chinese Philosophy*, Princeton: Princeton University Press, 1969: p. 500.

with the external world, consciousness and knowledge emerge. Only those who fully develop their nature can unify the state of formlessness and unaffectedness, and the state of objectification and affectedness.

Although material force in the universe integrates and disintegrates, and attracts and repulses in a hundred ways, nevertheless the principle ("li") according to which it operates has an order and is unerring.

天地之气，虽聚散、攻取百途，然其为理也顺而不妄。

As an entity, material force simply reverts to its original substance when it disintegrates and becomes formless. When it integrates and assumes form, it does not lose the eternal principle (of Change). The Great Vacuity of necessity consists of material force. Material force of necessity integrates to become the myriad things. Things of necessity disintegrate and return to the Great Vacuity. Appearance and disappearance following this cycle are a matter of necessity. When, in the midst [of this universal operation] the sage fulfills the Way to the utmost, and identifies himself [with the universal processes of appearance and disappearance] without partiality (i.e. lives the best life and takes life and death objectively), his spirit is preserved in the highest degree. Those (the Buddhists) who believe in annihilation expect departure without returning, and those (the Daoists) who cling to everlasting life and are attached to existence expect things not to change. While they differ, they are the same in failing to understand the Way.

气之为物，散入无形，适得吾体；聚为有象，不失吾常。太虚不能无气，气不能不聚而为万物，万物不能不散而为太虚。循是出入，是皆不得已而然也。

然则圣人尽道其间，兼体而不累者，存神其至矣。

彼语寂灭者往而不反，徇生执有者物而不化，二者虽有间矣，以言乎失道则均焉。

Whether integrated or disintegrated, it is my body just the same. One is qualified to discuss the nature of man when he realizes that death is not annihilation.[1]

聚亦吾体，散亦吾体，知死之不亡者，可与言性矣。

As the Great Vacuity, material force is extensive and vague. Yet it ascends and descends and moves in all ways

气坱然太虚，升降飞扬，未尝止息，易

---

1. Comment from the translator: As Zhang Boxing (1651–1725) has noted, to say that death is not annihilation is dangerously close to Buddhist transmigration. He quickly points out, however, that what Zhang meant is neither Buddhist transmigration nor Daoist immortality on earth but the indestructibility of material force whether it is integrated or disintegrated. What is not annihilated, then, is not the person but principle, according to which material force operates.

without ever ceasing. This is what is called in *The Book of Changes* "fusion and intermingling" and in the Zhuangzi "fleeting forces moving in all directions while all living beings blow against one another with their breath." Here lies the subtle, incipient activation of reality and unreality, of motion and rest, and the beginning of yin and yang, as well as the elements of strength and weakness. Yang that is clear ascends upward, whereas yin that is turbid sinks downward. As a result of their contact and influence and of their integration and disintegration, winds and rains, snow and frost come into being. Whether it be the countless variety of things in their changing configurations or the mountains and rivers in their fixed forms, the dregs of wine or the ashes of fire, there is nothing (in which the principle) is not revealed.

所謂"絪緼", 庄生所谓"生物以息相吹"、"野馬"者与！此虚实、动静之机, 阴阳、刚柔之始。浮而上者阳之清, 降而下者阴之浊, 其感遇聚结, 为风雨, 为雪霜, 万品之流形, 山川之融结, 糟粕煨烬, 无非教也。

The integration and disintegration of material force is to the Great Vacuity as the freezing and melting of ice is to water. If we realize that the Great Vacuity is identical with material Force, we know that there is no such thing as non-being. Therefore, when discussing the ultimate problems of the nature of things and the Way of Heaven, the sage limits himself to the marvelous changes and transformations of yin and yang and the Five Agents (of Metal, Wood, Water, Fire, and Earth). The doctrine of those superficial and mistaken philosophers who draw the distinction between being and non-being is not the way to investigate principle to the utmost.[1]

气之聚散于太虚, 犹冰凝释于水, 知太虚即气, 则无无。故圣人语性与天道之极, 尽于参伍之神变易而已。诸子浅妄, 有有无之分, 非穷理之学也。

It is according to one's nature that being and non-being, and reality and unreality pervade a thing. If they are not united as one, nature cannot be developed fully. Food

有无虚实通伪一物者, 性也; 不能为一, 非尽性也。饮食男女皆性也, 是乌可灭?

---

1. Comment from the translator: Zhang's theory of material force exercised considerable influence on Wang Fuzhi (1619–1692), whose philosophy of principle as inherent in material force is as materialistic as the philosophy of Zhang. It is easily understandable why Wang was an admirer of Zhang but a severe critic of Zhu Xi (朱熹) and Cheng Yi (程颐), who contrasted principle and material force too sharply to suit him. As to Zhang's own theory of material force, he has never explained why some is clear and some is turbid. Neither has he made his idea of the nature clear. For these, we have to wait till Cheng and Zhu.

and sex are both nature. How can they be obliterated? Thus being and non-being are both nature. How can there be no opposition? The Daoists and Buddhists have for long maintained that there is none. Do they really understand truth?

In trying to understand spirits, Buddhists say that beings with consciousness die and are born in cycles. They are therefore tired of suffering and seek to escape from it. Can they be said to understand spiritual beings? They consider human life as a delusion. Can they be said to understand man? Heaven and man form a unity, but they accept one (the ultimate nature of Heaven) and reject the other (human affairs). Can they be said to understand Heaven? What Confucius and Mencius called Heaven, they call the Path. "The wandering away of the spirit (material force) [as it disintegrates] becomes change," but the deluded Buddhists call this transmigration. They just don't think.[1]

然则有无皆性也，是岂无对？庄、老、浮屠为此说久矣，果畅真理乎？

浮屠明鬼，谓有识之死受生循环，遂厌苦求免，可谓知鬼乎？以人生为妄见，可谓知人乎？天人一物，辄生取舍，可谓知天乎？

孔孟所谓天，彼所谓道。惑者指游魂为变伪轮回，未之思也。

---

1. Comment from the translator: Neo-Confucians attacked Buddhism on all fronts. Zhang did so mostly on philosophical grounds. Other Neo-Confucianists, like Cheng Hao (程颢), Cheng Yi, and Wang Yangming (1472–1529), stressed the social and ethical aspects by emphasizing Buddhist escape from social responsibility and selfish desire for personal salvation.

An Excerpt from
The Problem of China[1]

Bertrand Russell

Confucius (551 BC–479 BC) must be reckoned, as regards his social influence, with the founders of religions. His effect on institutions and on men's thoughts has been of the same kind of magnitude as that of Buddha, Christ, or Muhammad, but curiously different in its nature. Unlike Buddha and Christ, he is a completely historical character, about whose life a great deal is known, and with whom legend and myth have been less busy than with most men of his kind. What most distinguishes him from other founders is that he inculcated a strict code of ethics, which has been respected ever since, but associated it with very little religious dogma, which gave place to complete theological skepticism in the countless generations of Chinese literati who revered his memory and administered the Empire.

Confucius himself belongs rather to the type of Lycurgus and Solon than to that of the great founders of religions. He was a practical statesman, concerned with the administration of the State; the virtues he sought to inculcate were not those of personal holiness, or designed to secure salvation in a future life, but rather those which lead to a peaceful and prosperous community here on earth. His outlook was essentially conservative, and aimed at preserving the virtues of former ages. He accepted the existing religion—a rather unemphatic monotheism, combined with belief that the spirits of the dead preserved a shadowy existence, which it was the duty of their descendants to render as comfortable as possible. He did not, however, lay any stress upon supernatural matters. In answer to a question, he gave the following definition of wisdom: "To cultivate earnestly our duty towards our neighbor, and to reverence spiritual beings while maintaining always a due reserve." But reverence for spiritual beings was not an active part of Confucianism, except in the form of ancestor-worship, which was part of filial piety, and thus merged in duty towards one's neighbor. Filial piety included obedience to the Emperor, except when he was so wicked as to forfeit his divine

---

1. Bertrand Russell, *The Problem of China*, London: Photolithography Unwin Brothers Limited, 1922.

right—for the Chinese, unlike the Japanese, have always held that resistance to the Emperor was justified if he governed very badly. The following passage from Professor Giles illustrates this point:

> The Emperor has been uniformly regarded as the son of God by adoption only, and liable to be displaced from that position as a punishment for the offense of misrule.... If the ruler failed in his duties, the obligation of the people was at an end, and his divine right disappeared simultaneously. Of this we have an example in a portion of the Canon to be examined by and by. Under the year 558 BC we find the following narrative. One of the feudal princes asked an official, saying, "Have not the people of the Wei State done very wrong in expelling their ruler?" "Perhaps the ruler himself," was the reply, "may have done very wrong.... If the life of the people is impoverished, and if the spirits are deprived of their sacrifices, of what use is the ruler, and what can the people do but get rid of him?"

This very sensible doctrine has been accepted at all times throughout Chinese history, and has made rebellions only too frequent.

Filial piety and the strength of the family generally, are perhaps the weakest point in Confucian ethics, the only point where the system departs seriously from common sense. Family feeling has militated against public spirit, and the authority of the old has increased the tyranny of ancient custom. In the present day, when China is confronted with problems requiring a radically new outlook, these features of the Confucian system have made it a barrier to necessary reconstruction, and accordingly we find all those foreigners who wish to exploit China praising the old tradition and deriding the efforts of Young China to construct something more suited to modern needs. The way in which Confucian emphasis on filial piety prevented the growth of public spirit is illustrated by the following story:

> One of the feudal princes was boasting to Confucius of the high level of morality which prevailed in his own State. "Among us here," he said, "you will find upright men. If a father has stolen a sheep, his son will give evidence against him." "In my part of the country," replied Confucius, "there is a different standard from this. A father will shield his son, a son will shield his father. It is thus that uprightness will be found."

It is interesting to contrast this story with that of the elder Brutus and his sons, upon which we in the West were all brought up.

Zhao Ji, expounding the Confucian doctrine, says it is contrary to filial piety to refuse a lucrative post by which to relieve the indigence of one's aged parents. This form of sin, however, is rare in China as in other countries.

The worst failure of filial piety, however, is to remain without children, since ancestors are supposed to suffer if they have no descendants to keep up their cult. It is probable that this doctrine has made the Chinese more prolific, in which case it has had great biological importance. Filial piety is, of course, in no way peculiar to China, but has been universal at a certain stage of culture. In this respect, as in certain others, what is peculiar to China is the preservation of the old custom after a very high level of civilization had been attained. The early Greeks and Romans did not differ from the Chinese in this respect, but as their civilization advanced the family became less and less important. In China, this did not begin to happen until our own day.

Whatever may be said against filial piety carried to excess, it is certainly less harmful than its Western counterpart, patriotism. Both, of course, err in inculcating duties to a certain portion of mankind to the practical exclusion of the rest. But patriotism directs one's loyalty to a fighting unit, which filial piety does not (except in a very primitive society). Therefore patriotism leads much more easily to militarism and imperialism. The principal method of advancing the interests of one's nation is homicide; the principal method of advancing the interest of one's family is corruption and intrigue. Therefore family feeling is less harmful than patriotism. This view is borne out by the history and present condition of China as compared to Europe.

Apart from filial piety, Confucianism was, in practice, mainly a code of civilized behavior, degenerating at times into an etiquette book. It taught self-restraint, moderation, and above all courtesy. Its moral code was not, like those of Buddhism and Christianity, so severe that only a few saints could hope to live up to it, or so much concerned with personal salvation as to be incompatible with political institutions. It was not difficult for a man of the world to live up to the more imperative parts of the Confucian teaching. But in order to do this he must exercise at all times a certain kind of self-control—an extension of the kind which children learn when they are taught to "behave." He must not break into violent passions; he must not be arrogant; he must "save face," and never inflict humiliations upon defeated adversaries; he must be moderate in all things, never carried away by excessive love or hate; in a word, he must keep calm reason always in control of all his actions. This attitude existed in Europe in the eighteenth century, but perished in the French Revolution romanticism, Rousseau, and the guillotine put an end to it. In China, though wars and revolutions have occurred constantly, Confucian calm has survived them all, making them less terrible for the participants, and making all who were not immediately involved hold aloof. It is bad manners in China to attack your adversary in wet weather. Wu Peifu, I am told, once did it, and won a victory; the beaten general complained of the breach of etiquette; so Wu Peifu went back to the position he held before the battle, and fought all over again on a fine day. (It should be said that battles in China are seldom bloody.) In such a country, militarism is not the scourge it is with us; and the difference is due to the Confucian ethics.

Confucianism did not assume its present form until the twelfth century AD, when the personal God in whom Confucius had believed was thrust aside by the philosopher Zhu Fuzi, whose interpretation of Confucianism has ever since been recognized as orthodox. Since the fall of the Mongols (1370), the Government has uniformly favored Confucianism as the teaching of the State; before that, there were struggles with Buddhism and Daoism, which were connected with magic, and appealed to superstitious Emperors, quite a number of whom died of drinking the Daoist elixir of life. The Mongol Emperors were Buddhists of the Lama religion, which still prevails in Tibet and Mongolia; but the Manchu Emperors, though also northern conquerors, were ultra-orthodox Confucians. It has been customary in China, for many centuries, for the literati to be pure Confucians, skeptical in religion but not in morals, while the rest of the population believed and practiced all three religions simultaneously. The Chinese have not the belief, which we owe to the Jews, that if one religion is true, all others must be false. At the present day, however, there appears to be very little in the way of religion in China, though the belief in magic lingers on among the uneducated. At all times, even when there was religion, its intensity was far less than in Europe. It is remarkable that religious skepticism has not led, in China, to any corresponding ethical skepticism, as it has done repeatedly in Europe.

I come now to the system of selecting officials by competitive examination, without which it is hardly likely that so literary and unsuperstitious a system as that of Confucius could have maintained its hold. The view of the modern Chinese on this subject is set forth by the present President of "the Republic of China," Xu Shichang, in his book on China after the War, pp. 59–60. After considering the educational system under the Chou dynasty, he continues:

> In later periods, in spite of minor changes, the importance of moral virtues continued to be stressed upon. For instance, during the most flourishing period of Tang Dynasty (627 AD–650 AD), the Imperial Academy of Learning, known as Guo Zi Jian, was composed of four collegiate departments, in which ethics was considered as the most

important of all studies. It was said that in the Academy there were more than three thousand students who were able and virtuous in nearly all respects, while the total enrollment, including aspirants from Korea and Japan, was as high as eight thousand. At the same time, there was a system of "elections" through which able and virtuous men were recommended by different districts to the Emperor for appointment to public offices. College training and local elections supplemented each other, but in both moral virtues were given the greatest emphasis.

Although the Imperial Academy exists till this day, it has never been as nourishing as during that period. For this change the introduction of the competitive examination or Ke Ju system, must be held responsible. The "election" system furnished no fixed standard for the recommendation of public service candidates, and, as a result, tended to create an aristocratic class from which alone were to be found eligible men. Consequently, the Sung Emperors (960 AD–1277 AD) abolished the elections, set aside the Imperial Academy, and inaugurated the competitive examination system in their place. The examinations were to supply both scholars and practical statesmen, and they were periodically held throughout the later dynasties until the introduction of the modern educational regime. Useless and stereotyped as they were in later days, they once served some useful purpose. Besides, the ethical background of Chinese education had already been so firmly established, that, in spite of the emphasis laid by these examinations on pure literary attainments, moral teachings have survived till this day in family education and in private schools.

Although the system of awarding Government posts for proficiency in examinations is much better than most other systems that have prevailed, such as nepotism, bribery, threats of insurrection, etc., yet the Chinese system, at any rate after it assumed its final form, was harmful through the fact that it was based solely on the classics, that it was purely literary, and that it allowed no scope whatever for originality.

The system was established in its final form by the Emperor Hong Wu (1368 AD–1398 AD), and remained unchanged until 1905. One of the first objects of modern Chinese reformers was to get it swept away. Li Weng Bing says:

In spite of the many good things that may be said to the credit of Hung Wu, he will ever be remembered in connection with a form of evil which has eaten into the very heart of the nation. This was the system of triennial examinations, or rather the form of Chinese composition, called the "Essay," or the "Eight Legs," which, for the first time in the history of Chinese literature, was made the basis of all literary contests. It was so-named, because after the introduction of the theme the writer was required to treat it in four paragraphs, each consisting of two members, made up of an equal number of sentences and words. The theme was always chosen from either the Four Books, or the Five Classics. The writer could not express any opinion of his own, or any views at variance with those expressed by Zhu Xi and his school. All he was required to do was to put the few words of Confucius, or whomsoever it might be, into an essay in conformity with the prescribed rules. Degrees, which were to serve as passports to Government positions, were awarded the best writers. To say that the training afforded by the time required to make a man efficient in the art of such writing, would at the same time qualify him to hold the various offices under the Government, was absurd. But absurd as the whole system was, it was handed down to recent times from the third year of the reign of Hung Wu, and was not abolished until a few years ago. No system was more perfect or effective in retarding the intellectual and literary development of a nation. With her "Eight Legs," China long ago reached the lowest point on her downhill journey. It is largely on account of the long lease of life that was granted to this rotten system that the teachings of the Sung philosophers have been so long venerated.

These are the words of a Chinese patriot of the present day, and no doubt, as a modern system, the "Eight Legs" deserve all the hard things that he says about them. But in the fourteenth century, when one considers the practicable alternatives, one can see that there was probably much to be said for such a plan. At any rate, for good or evil, the examination system profoundly affected the civilization of China. Among its good effects were: A widely-diffused respect for learning; the possibility of doing without a hereditary aristocracy; the selection of administrators who must at least have been capable of industry; and the preservation of Chinese civilization in spite of barbarian conquest. But, like so much else in traditional China, it has had to be swept away to meet modern needs. I hope nothing of greater value will have to perish in the struggle to repel the foreign exploiters and the fierce and cruel system which they miscall civilization.

Study Questions

1. Relate Confucius's own life with what he said about loyalty (忠), then tell what kind of a loyalty he meant? And how does that respond to what he said about reciprocity (恕)?

2. Since both Mencius and Xunzi emphasized on the cultivation of virtue, please use some quotes to evidence such a proposition. Then explain how this point reveals the feature of the Confucian learning?

3. How do you understand what Mencius believed about the nature of human beings? To what extent do you agree with it?

4. Some scholars argued that Xunzi proclaimed a hegemonic ruling, which seemed to go against the Confucian ideal of benevolent governance. How do you explain such a paradox as arguable in Xunzi's thoughts?

5. Mencius says, "The will is the leader of the vital force, and the vital force pervades and animates the body. The will is the highest; the vital force comes next. Therefore I say, 'Hold the will firm and never do violence to the vital force.'" ("夫志, 气之帅也; 气, 体之充也。夫志至焉, 气次焉, 故曰: '持其志, 无暴其气'"。《孟子·公孙丑上》) Relate it to the passage excerpted in this chapter in which Mencius explains the "vast vital energy," and figure out a metaphor to describe the relationship between "will" (志) and "vital energy" (气).

6. According to Aristotle's theology, a form of invariant form exists without matter, beyond the cosmos, powerless and oblivious, in the eternal substance of the unmoved movent, which paradoxically causes the continuous motion of the world of things. Compare such an idea as embedded in the following passage from Aristotle's Physics with the concept of "Non-Ultimate" as theorized by Zhou Dunyi.

   "Resuming our main argument, we proceed from the positions that there must be continuous motion in the world of things, that this is a single motion, that a single motion must be a motion of a magnitude (for that which is without magnitude cannot be in motion), and that the magnitude must be a single magnitude moved by a single movent (for otherwise there will not be continuous motion but a consecutive series of separate motions), and that if the movement is a single thing, it is either itself in motion or itself unmoved: if, then, it is in motion, it will have to be subject to the same conditions as that which it moves, that is to say it will itself be in process of change and in being so will also have to be moved by something: so we have a series that must come to an end, and a point will be reached at which motion is imparted by something that is unmoved. Thus we have a movent that has no need to change along with that which it moves but will be able to cause motion always (for the causing of motion under these conditions involves no effort): and this motion alone is regular, or at least it is so in a higher degree than any other, since the movent is never subject to any change. So, too, in order that the motion may continue to be of the same character, the moved must not be subject to change in respect of its relation to the movent. Moreover the movent must occupy either the center or the circumference, since these are the first principles from which a sphere is derived. But the things nearest the movent are those whose motion is quickest, and in this case it is the motion of the circumference that is the quickest: therefore the movent occupies the circumference. There is a further difficulty in supposing it to be possible for anything that is in motion to cause motion continuously and not merely in the way in which it is caused by something repeatedly pushing (in which case the continuity amounts to no more than successiveness). Such a movent must either itself continue to push or pull or perform both these actions, or else the action must be taken up by something else and be passed on from one movent to another (the process that we described before as occurring in the case of things thrown, since the air or the water, being divisible, is a movent only in virtue of the fact that different parts of the air are moved one after another): and in either case the motion cannot be a single motion, but only a consecutive series of motions. The only continuous motion, then, is that which is caused by the unmoved movent: and this motion is continuous because the movent remains always invariable, so that its relation to that which it moves remains also invariable and continuous.

Now that these points are settled, it is clear that the first unmoved movent cannot have any magnitude. For if it has magnitude, this must be either a finite or an infinite magnitude. Now we have already proved in our course on Physics that there cannot be an infinite magnitude: and we have now proved that it is impossible for a finite magnitude to have an infinite force, and also that it is impossible for a thing to be moved by a finite magnitude during an infinite time. But the first movent causes a motion that is eternal and does cause it during an infinite time. It is clear, therefore, that the first movent is indivisible and is without parts and without magnitude."

7. Compare two poems on autumn, and relate the comparison to the Confucian idealization of the sagely character, then figure out the following questions.

a) Which poem reveals the "character" of heaven and earth, the "brightness" of sun and moon, and the sense of order of the four seasons?

b) How does this comparison help you understand the idea of "focusing on the tranquility" (主静) or "without desire" (无欲)?

Autumn Day

Rainer Maria Rilke (Germany)

Lord: it is time. The summer was immense.
Lay your shadow on the sundials
And let loose the wind in the fields.
Bid the last fruits to be full;
Give them another two more southerly days,
Press them to ripeness, and chase
The last sweetness into the heavy wine.
Whoever has no house now will not build one anymore.
Whoever is alone now will remain so for a long time,
Will stay up, read, write long letters,
And wander the avenues, up and down,
Restlessly, while the leaves are blowing.

秋风辞

刘彻(汉武帝)

秋风起兮白云飞,
草木黄落兮雁南归。
兰有秀兮菊有芳,
怀佳人兮不能忘。
泛楼船兮济汾河,
横中流兮扬素波。
箫鼓鸣兮发棹歌,
欢乐极兮哀情多。

CHAPTER ❸

Philosophical Daoism and Its Imaginativeness

Pre-reading Questions

1. When trying to define what "beauty" is, people come up with different views and standards. If you do a little research on the aesthetic discussions of this concept, you will find that the different conceptual frames to look at such a concept even make the discussion messier. How do you explain such a situation that we often find ourselves in?

2. The American writer Paul Eldridge once said, in a rather cynical manner, "Man is ready to die for an idea, provided that the idea is not quite clear to him." If Confucius and Zhuangzi lived to know such a statement, what do you think would be their response?

Introduction

Both Confucians and Daoists are idealists, yet they believe in different ideals. While Confucianism strives for an ethical construction within the human realm, straightening out a rational hierarchy of social relations, philosophical Daoism, by aspiring for a spiritual transcendence degrading socialized standards, believes in the power of nature to bring bliss to the human being. Thus, complementing each other, Confucianism and Daoism enrich Chinese classical culture with a dialectical tension and tolerance for varieties.

Both Confucianism and Daoism aim at a kind of balance—a harmony in which one makes peace with the world. The difference lies in the fact that Confucianism strives to make peace with the external world, the society and its ethical regulations, while Daoism attempts to educate one to make peace with his inner world—both his physical and mental states of being.

In Daoism, there is a conspicuous relativism as Laozi sees the relative nature of things. He believes that if people are exposed to what is moral and legal, then they surely know what is immoral and illegal. Zhuangzi goes further by looking at the harm inflicted upon a single person's state of being if he clings to what is moral and right. In our selected reading of *Zhuangzi*, the auther tells of stories where people would rather die to earn a reputation of morality. And Zhuangzi absolutely disapproves of such a kind of stubbornness. So to the Daoist, it is more important to make peace with oneself instead of the external world. This is because the standards or values set up in the external world tend to interrupt the inner harmony of a person's own being. They believe in following the natural way of things. And such a view is not necessarily pessimistic, as mistaken by many people. Because what is natural is often blinded by what is unnaturally built up in our world. And to see through the unnatural and even false values is in and of itself an intellectual endeavor one needs to keep throughout his life.

Another contrast that parts the two schools is their clashing ideas on "name," or to put it more precisely, the terministic power of language in defining and prescribing the way of things. Though both hold that to name the myriad things in this world establishes the very foundation of human civilization, Confucianism seeks to correct the names that clarify interpersonal relations so that people are confined within their granted positions prescribed by Confucian ethics; Daoism, after claiming that to name is to bring everything into existence, wittily points out that things, as the way that produces them originally, have their nature escaping from us the moment we have defined them with names.

Among all the Confucian ideals and models, one that has been most influential in shaping Chinese spirit is an idealization of the character of the "sage" or "sagely" human being, which becomes one of the main targets of the Daoist defiance. Laozi started the explanation with the concept of beauty, confirming that the grand beauty never speaks for itself. As a classical Chinese logic, the idea of beauty easily extends to the idea of morality, hence Laozi went on in his terse verse that "He who speaks about morality, is most questionable of his own morality." So based on the Daoist theory of reversing, moral talking may produce moral hypocrisy. Modern ethics actually finds its conformity or even enlightenment with Laozi, especially in the concept of "Moral Licensing." The idea is that if one keeps considering himself as being moral consciously, he may instead license himself to impair his moral behaviors.

If *Laozi* was written in a fairly concise and reserved way to indicate the possibility neglected by Confucianism, then Zhuangzi presented stories, allegories, and allusions with more vitality, humor, and vividness. Historical figures honored in a Confucian tradition, the loyal officials, filial sons, and even Confucians, were reviewed and revalued in *Zhuangzi*'s brilliant humor. *Zhuangzi*'s disagreement of Confucianism is implicitly weaved into allegorical accounts and enlightening statements, without any showiness or aggressiveness, the rhetorical feature being a representation of the Daoist aloofness and disinterestedness. Yet this does not detach *Zhuangzi* from us, instead, this lack of antagonism against the predominance of Confucianism as sensed in the Daoist writings, attracts a consistent flow of readers throughout Chinese history with its breath of wisdom and expanse of imaginativeness.

Selected Passages from *Dao De Jing*[1]

Laozi

Chapter One

The Dao that can be defined is not the real Dao.

The name that can be named is not the real Name.

The unnamable [Dao] is the source of Heaven and Earth.

Naming is the mother of all particular things.

Free from desire, you experience reality.

Trapped in desire, you see only appearances.

Reality and appearance have different names,

but they emerge from the same source [i.e. the Dao].

This source is called darkness, deep darkness;

and yet it is the way to all wisdom.

Chapter Two

No beauty without ugliness.

No good without evil.

Being and non–being are two aspects of the same reality.

Difficult and easy, long and short, high and low, before and after:

With each pair, two sides of the same coin.

Therefore, the Dao-Master acts with non-ado [wu-wei] and teaches without speaking.

Things come and go. He lets them come and go.

He creates, but he does not own.

He achieves, but he takes no credit.

He completes his work and then forgets about it.

Practice non–ado, and your accomplishments endure.

《道德经》选篇

老子

第一章

道可道，非常道。
名可名，非常名。
无名天地之始。
有名万物之母。
故常无欲以观其妙。
常有欲以观其徼。
此两者同出而异名，
同谓之玄。
玄之又玄，
众妙之门。

第二章

天下皆知美之为
美，斯恶矣；
皆知善之为善，斯
不善已。故有无相生，
难易相成，长短相形，
高下相倾，音声相和，
前后相随。
是以圣人处无为之
事，行不言之教。
万物作焉而不辞。
生而不有，
为而不恃，
功成而弗居。
夫唯弗居，是以不
去。

---

1. Cronk, George, *Readings in Philosophy: Eastern & Western Sources*, Plymouth: Hayden-McNeil Publishing, 1999.

Chapter Nine

Fill your bowl all the way: it overflows.

    Keep sharpening your sword: it gets dull.

    Pile up gold and jade: it cannot be protected.

    Increase your wealth, status, and power: you suffer ruin.

    Do your work, then withdraw: that's the Way!

Chapter Twenty-Nine

Know the male, maintain the female: become the channel of all things.

    Become the channel of all things, and true power [De] will endure.

    You will be reborn.

    Know the white, maintain the black: become the form of all things.

    Become the form of all things, and true power [De] will endure.

    You will return to the Infinite.

    Know honor, maintain humility: become the valley of all things.

    Become the valley of all things, and true power [De] will endure.

    You will find the simplicity of nature.

    Uncarved wood, when carved by the Dao–Master, becomes a well-governed state.

    The best carving is that which is not carved at all.

Chapter Thirty-Eight

The Dao-Master does not cling to power and is therefore truly powerful.

    The lesser man clings to power and thus has none.

    The truly powerful man does nothing [i.e. he practices nonado (wu-wei)] and thus leaves nothing undone.

    The lesser man is awhirl with activity and thus gets nothing accomplished.

    The virtuous man does what is good as an end in itself.

第九章
持而盈之，不如其已；
揣而锐之，不可长保；
金玉满堂，莫之能守；
富贵而骄，自遗其咎。
功遂身退，天之道。

第二十八章
知其雄，守其雌，
为天下溪。
    为天下溪，常德不离，
    复归于婴儿。
    知其白，守其黑，
为天下式。
    为天下式，常德不忒，
    复归于无极。
    知其荣，守其辱，
为天下谷。
    为天下谷，常德乃足，
    复归于朴。
    朴散则为器，圣人用之则为官长。
    故大制不割。

第三十八章
    上德不德，是以有德。
    下德不失德，是以无德。
    上德无为而无以为。
    下德无为而有以为。
    上仁为之而无以为。

The moral man has a need to do what is good.

The man of propriety (li) makes doing good into a ritual, and if people do not follow him willingly, he forces them into line.

Thus, when the Dao is lost, virtue arises.

When virtue is lost, morality arises.

When morality is lost, justice arises.

When justice is lost, propriety arises.

Propriety is merely a shadow of justice, morality, and virtue; it is the beginning of chaos ...

Therefore, the Dao-Master stays with the Dao.

He does not live on the surface of things.

He looks to the fruit, not to the flower.

He accepts this [Dao] and rejects that [non-Dao].

上义为之而有以
为。

上礼为之而莫之以
应，则攘臂而扔之。
故失道而后德。
失德而后仁。
失仁而后义。
失义而后礼。
夫礼者忠信之薄而
乱之首。……

是以大丈夫，处其
厚不居其薄。
处其实，不居其
华。故去彼取此。

Chapter Sixty-Three

第六十三章

Act without ado; work without effort.

Taste the tasteless; treat the small as large and the few as many.

Reward evil with goodness.

Take on the difficult while it is still easy, the large while it is still small.

Difficult always begins as easy; large always begins as small.

Therefore, the Dao–Master never tries to be great.

As a result, he accomplishes great things.

Big promises produce little trust.

Treating something as quite easy makes it very difficult.

The Dao–Master regards everything as difficult, which means that, for him, everything is easy.

为无为，事无事，
味无味。大小多
少，
报怨以德。
图难於其易，为大
于其细。天下难事必作
于易。天下大事必作于
细。
是以圣人终不为
大，故能成其大。
夫轻诺必寡信。
多易必多难。

是以圣人犹难之，
故终无难矣。

"External Things" from *Zhuangzi*[1]

《庄子·外物》
选篇

External things cannot be counted on. Hence Longpang was executed, Bi Gan was sentenced to death, Prince Ji feigned madness, E Lai was killed, and Jie and Zhou were overthrown. There is no ruler who does not want his ministers to be loyal. But loyal ministers are not always trusted. Hence Wu Yuan was thrown into the Yangtze and Chang Hong died in Shu, where the people stored away his blood, and after three years it was transformed into green jade. There is no parent who does not want his son to be filial. But filial sons are not always loved. Hence Xiaoji grieved and Zeng Shen sorrowed.

外物不可必，故龙逢诛，比干戮，箕子狂，恶来死，桀纣亡。人主莫不欲其臣之忠，而忠未必信，故伍员流于江，苌弘死于蜀，藏其血，三年而化为碧。人亲莫不欲其子之孝，而孝未必爱，故孝己忧而曾参悲。

When metal rubs against wood, flames spring up. When metal remains by the side of fire, it melts and flows away. When the yin and yang go awry, then heaven and earth see astounding sights. Then we hear the crash and roll of thunder, and fire comes in the midst of rain and burns up the great pagoda tree. Delight and sorrow are there to trap man on either side so that he has no escape. Fearful and trembling, he can reach no completion. His mind is as though trussed and suspended between heaven and earth, bewildered and lost in delusion. Profit and loss rub against each other and light the countless fires that burn up the inner harmony of the mass of men. The moon cannot put out the fire, so that in time all is consumed and the Way comes to an end.

金与木相摩则然，金与火相守则流。阴阳错行，则天地大骇，于是乎有雷有霆，水中有火，乃焚大槐。有甚忧两陷而无所逃，螴蜳不得成，心若悬于天地之间。慰㬳沈屯，则利害相摩，生火甚多众人焚和。月固不胜火，于是乎有僓然而道尽。

Zhuang Zhou's family was very poor and so he went to borrow some grain from the marquis of Jianhou. The marquis said, "Why, of course. I'll soon be getting the tribute money from my fief, and when I do, I'll be glad to lend you three hundred pieces of gold. Will that be all right?"

庄周家贫，故往贷粟于监河侯。监河侯曰："诺。我将得邑金，将贷子三百金，可乎？"

---

1. Translated by Burton Watson and excerpted from http://web. archive.org/web/20041011153535/http://users.compaqnet.be/cn111132/Zhuang-tzu/26.htm

Zhuang Zhou flushed with anger and said, "As I was coming here yesterday, I heard someone calling me on the road. I turned around and saw that there was a perch in the carriage rut. I said to him, 'Come, perch—what are you doing here?' He replied, 'I am a Wave Official of the Eastern Sea. Couldn't you give me a dipperful of water, so I can stay alive?' I said to him, 'Why, of course. I'm just about to start south to visit the kings of Wu and Yue. I'll change the course of the West River and send it in your direction. Will that be all right?' The perch flushed with anger and said, 'I've lost my element! I have nowhere to go! If you can get me a dipper of water, I'll be able to stay alive. But if you give me an answer like that, then you'd best look for me in the dried fish store!'"

Prince Ren made an enormous fishhook with a huge line, baited it with fifty bullocks, settled himself on top of Mount Kuaiji, and cast with his pole into the eastern sea. Morning after morning he dropped the hook, but for a whole year he got nothing. At last a huge fish swallowed the bait, and dived down, dragging the enormous hook. It plunged to the bottom in a fierce charge, rose up and shook its dorsal fins, until the white waves were like mountains and the sea waters lashed and churned. The noise was like that of gods and demons and it spread terror for a thousand li. When Prince Ren had landed his fish, he cut it up and dried it, and from Zhihe east, from Cangwu north, there was no one who did not get his fill. Since then the men of later generations who have piddling talents and a penchant for odd stories all astound each other by repeating the tale.

Now if you shoulder your pole and line, march to the ditches and gullies, and watch for minnows and perch, then you'll have a hard time ever landing a big fish. If you parade your little theories and fish for the post of district magistrate, you will be far from the Great Understanding. So if a man has never heard of the style of Prince Ren, he's a long way from being able to join with the men who run the world. ...

庄周忿然作色曰：“周昨来，有中道而呼者。周顾视车辙中，有鲋鱼焉。周问之曰：'鲋鱼，来！子何为者邪？'对曰：'我，东海之波臣也。君岂有斗升之水而活我哉？'周曰：'诺。我且南游吴越之土，激西江之水而迎子，可乎？'鲋鱼忿然作色曰：'吾失我常与，我无所处。吾得斗升之水然活耳，君乃言此，曾不如早索我于枯鱼之肆！'"

任公子为大钩巨缁，五十犗以为饵，蹲乎会稽，投竿东海，旦旦而钓，期年不得鱼。已而，大鱼食之，牵巨钩，陷没而下；警扬而奋鳍，白波若山，海水震荡，声侔鬼神，惮赫千里。任公子得若鱼，离而腊之。自制河以东，苍梧以北，莫不厌若鱼者。已而后世辁才讽说之徒，皆惊而相告也。

夫揭竿累，趣灌渎，守鲵鲋，其于得大鱼，难矣。饰小说以干县令，其于大达亦远矣。是以未尝闻任氏之风俗，其不可与经于世，亦远矣。……

Lord Yuan of Song one night dreamed he saw a man with disheveled hair who peered in at the side door of his chamber and said, "I come from the Zai-lu Deeps. I was on my way as envoy from the Clear Yangtze to the court of the Lord of the Yellow River when a fisherman named Yu Chu caught me!"

When Lord Yuan woke up, he ordered his men to divine the meaning, and they replied, "This is a sacred turtle." "Is there a fisherman named Yu Chu?" he asked, and his attendants replied, "There is." "Order Yu Chu to come to court!" he said.

The next day Yu Chu appeared at court and the ruler said, "What kind of fish have you caught recently?"

Yu Chu replied, "I caught a white turtle in my net. It's five feet around." "Present your turtle!" ordered the ruler. When the turtle was brought, the ruler could not decide whether to kill it or let it live and, being in doubt, he consulted his diviners, who replied, "Kill the turtle and divine with it—it will bring good luck." Accordingly the turtle was stripped of its shell, and of seventy-two holes drilled in it for prognostication, not one failed to yield a true answer.

Confucius said, "The sacred turtle could appear to Lord Yuan in a dream but it couldn't escape from Yu Chu's net. It knew enough to give correct answers to seventy-two queries but it couldn't escape the disaster of having its belly ripped open. So it is that knowledge has its limitations, and spirituality has that which it can do nothing about. Even the most perfect wisdom can be outwitted by ten thousand schemers. Fish do not [know enough to] fear a net, but only to fear pelicans. Discard little wisdom and great wisdom will become clear. Discard goodness and goodness will come of itself. The little child learns to speak, though it has no learned teachers—because it lives with those who know how to speak." ...

There was a man of Yen Gate who, on the death of his parents, won praise by starving and disfiguring himself, and was rewarded with the post of Official Teacher. The other people of the village likewise starved and disfigured

宋元君夜半而梦人被发窥阿门，曰："予自宰路之渊，予为清江使河伯之所，渔者余且得予。"

元君觉，使人占之，曰："此神龟也。"君曰："渔者有余且乎？"左右曰："有。"君曰："令余且会朝。"

明日，余且朝。君曰："渔何得？"

对曰："且之网得白龟焉，其圆五尺，"君曰："献若之龟。"龟至，君再欲杀之，再欲活之，心疑，卜之，曰："杀龟以卜吉。"乃刳龟，七十二钻而无遗。

仲尼曰："神龟能见梦于元君，而不能避余且之网；知能七十二钻而无遗，不能避刳肠之患。如是，则知有所困，神有所不及也。虽有至知，万人谋之。鱼不畏网而畏鹈鹕。去小知而大知明，去善而自善矣。婴儿生无石师而能言，与能言者处也。" ……

演门有亲死者，以善毁爵为官师，其党人毁而死者半。

themselves, and over half of them died. Yao offered the empire to Xu You and Xu You fled from him. Tang offered it to Wu Kuang and Wu Kuang railed at him. When Ji Tuo heard of this, he took his disciples and went off to sit by the Kuan River, where the feudal lords went to console him for three years. Shentu Di for the same reason jumped into the Yellow River.

The fish trap exists because of the fish; once you've gotten the fish, you can forget the trap. The rabbit snare rabbit, you can forget the snare. Words exist because of meaning; once you've gotten the meaning, you can forget the words. Where can I find a man who has forgotten words so I can have a word with him?

尧与许由天下，由逃之；汤与务光，务光怒之。纪他闻之，帅弟子而踆于窾水；诸侯吊之，三年，申徒狄因以踣河。

荃者所以在鱼，得鱼而忘荃；蹄者所以在兔，得兔而忘蹄；言者所以在意，得意而忘言。吾安得夫忘言之人而与之言哉！

Selected Passages from *On the Nourishment of Life*

Ji Kang[1]

《答难养生论》选篇

嵇康

Obey laws and follow principles so as not to fall into the net [of the law]. Honor the self for its freedom from crime, and enjoy peaceful leisure in the lack of burden. Roam in the realm of truth and righteousness, and lie down and rest in a humble abode. Be quiet, be at ease, and have nothing to thwart your wishes, and then your spirit and vital force will be in harmonious order. Is it necessary to have glory and splendor before one has honor? Cultivate the field to raise food and weave silk for clothing. When these are sufficient, leave the wealth of the world alone. Do as a thirsty person drinking from a river. He drinks happily enough, but does not covet the voluminous flow. Does one have to depend on an accumulation to be wealthy? This is how the gentleman exercises his mind for he regards rank and position as a tumor and material wealth as dirt and dust. What is the use of wealth and honor to him?

What is difficult to acquire in the world is neither wealth nor glory, but a sense of contentment. If one is contented, though he has only a small plot to cultivate, a coarse garment to wear, and beans to eat, in no case is he not satisfied. If one is discontented, though the whole world supports him and all things serve him, he is still not gratified. Thus it is that the contented needs nothing from the outside whereas the discontented needs everything from the outside. Needing everything, he is always in want no matter where he goes. Needing nothing, he lacks nothing regardless of splendor and glory, nor chase after vulgarity because he lives in obscurity, but moves

奉法循理, 不世网, 以无罪自尊, 以不仕为逸; 游心乎道义, 偃息乎卑室, 恬愉无遌, 而神气条达, 岂须荣华然后乃贵哉? 耕而为食, 蚕而为衣, 衣食周身, 则余天下之财, 犹渴者饮河, 快然以足, 不羡洪流, 岂待积敛然后乃富哉? 君子之用心若此, 盖将以名位为赘瘤, 资财为尘垢也, 安用富贵乎?

故世之难得者, 非财也, 非荣也。患意之不足耳! 意足者, 虽耦耕甽亩, 被褐啜菽, 岂不自得? 不足者, 虽养以天下, 委以万物, 犹未惬。然则足者不须外, 不足者无外之不须也。无不须, 故无往而不乏; 无所须, 故无适而不足。不以荣华肆志, 不以隐约趋俗,

---

1. WM. Theodore de Bary, Wing-Tsit Chan, and Burton Watson, *Sources of Chinese Tradition*, New York: Columbia University Press, 1960, p. 248.

and has his being with all things as one and cannot be either favored or disgraced, he is then really honored and wealthy. ... This is what the Laozi means when it says: "There is no greater happiness than freedom from worry, and there is no greater wealth than contentment."

混乎与万物并行，不可宠辱，此真有富贵也。……故老子曰："乐莫大于无忧，富莫大于知足。"此之谓也。

Extensive Reading A

Introduction to Painting[1]

叙画

Wang Wei[2]

王微(南朝宋)

People who discuss painting merely concentrate on the outward aspects and structural effects. Men of ancient times, however, when they produced paintings did not merely record the sites of cities, delineate country districts, mark out the boundaries of towns and villages, or sketch the courses of rivers. Physical appearances are based upon physical forms, but the mind is changing and ever active. But spirit is invisible, and therefore what it enters into does not move. The eye is limited in scope, and therefore what it sees does not cover all. Thus, by using one small brush, I draw the infinite vacuity [the universe in its undifferentiated state], and by employing the clear vision of my small pupils to the limit, I paint a large body. With a curved line I represent the Song mountain ranges. With an interesting line I represent [the mythical mountain] Fangzhang. A swift stroke will be sufficient for the Taihua Mountain, and some irregular dots will show a dragon's nose. [In the latter], the eyebrows, forehead, and cheeks all seem to be a serene smile, and [in the former], the lonely cliff is so luxuriant and sublime that it seems to emit clouds.

With changes and variations in all directions, movement is created, and by applying proportions and measure, the spirit is revealed. After this, things like the temples and shrines, and boats and carriages are grouped together according to kind, and creatures like dogs, horses,

夫言绘画者，竟求容势而已。且古人之作画也，非以案城域，辩方州，标镇阜，划浸流，本乎形者融，灵而动者变。

心止灵亡见，故所托不动；目有所极，故所见不周。于是乎以一管之笔拟太虚之体，以判躯之状画寸眸之明。

曲以为嵩高，趣以为方丈。以及之画，齐乎太华，枉之点表。夫隆准眉额颊辅，若晏笑兮，孤岩郁秀，若吐云兮。

横变纵化，故动生焉。前矩后方，而灵出焉，然后宫观舟车，器以类聚；犬马禽鱼，物以状分。此画之致也。

---

1. WM. Theodore de Bary, Wing-Tsit Chan, and Burton Watson. *Sources of Chinese Tradition,* New York: Columbia University Press, 1960, p. 252.
2. Wang Wei (415 AD–443 AD), painter in The Liu Song dynasty.

birds, and fish are distinguished according to their shape.
This is the ultimate of painting.

Gazing upon the clouds of autumn, my spirit takes
wings and soars. Facing the breeze of spring, my thoughts
flow like great, powerful currents. Even the music of
metal and stone instruments and the treasure of priceless
jade cannot match [the pleasure] of this. I unroll pictures
and examine documents, I compare and distinguish
the mountains and seas. The wind rises from the green
forest, and foaming water rushes in the stream. Alas! Such
paintings cannot be achieved by the physical movements
of the fingers and the hand, but only by the spirit entering
into them. This is the nature of painting.

望秋云，神飞扬，
临春风，思浩荡。虽有
金石之乐，圭璋之琛，
岂能仿佛之哉？披图按
牒，效异山海，绿林扬
风，白水激涧。呜呼!
岂独运诸指掌，亦以明
神降之，此画之情也。

Selected Passages from *Commentary on Zhuangzi*[1]

Guo Xiang

It is he who does no governing that can govern the empire. Therefore Yao governed by not governing. It was not because of his governing that his empire was governed. Now (the recluse) Xu You only realized that since the empire was well governed, he should not replace Yao. He thought it was Yao who did the actual governing. Consequently he said to Yao, "You govern the empire." He should have forgotten such words and investigated into that condition of peace. Someone may say, "It was Yao who actually governed and put the empire in good order but it was Xu You who enabled Yao to do so by refusing to govern himself." This is a great mistake. Yao was an adequate example of governing by not governing and acting by not acting. Why should we have to resort to Xu You? Are we to insist that a man fold his arms and sit in silence in the middle of some mountain forest before we will say he is practicing nonaction? This is why the words of Laozi and Zhuangzi are rejected by responsible officials. This is why responsible officials insist on remaining in the realm of action without regret. ... For egotistical people set themselves up against things, whereas he who is in accord with things is not opposed to them. ... Therefore he profoundly and deeply responds to things without any deliberate mind of his own and follows whatever comes into contact with him. He is like an untied boat drifting, claiming neither the east nor the west to be its own. He

---

1. Wing-Tsit Chan, *A Source Book in Chinese Philosophy*, Princeton: Princeton University Press, 1969, p. 327.

《庄子注》选篇

郭象

　　夫能令天下治，不治天下者也。故尧以不治治之，非治之而治者也。今许由方明既治，则无所代之。而治实由尧，故有子治之言。宜忘言以寻其所况。而或者遂云："治之而治者，尧也;不治而尧得以治者,许由也。"斯失之远矣。夫治之由乎不治，为之出乎无为也。取于尧而足，岂借之许由哉! 若谓拱默乎山林之中而后得称无为者，此庄老之谈所以见弃于当涂，[当涂]者自必于有为之域而不反者，斯之由也。……夫自任者，对物而顺物者，与物无对。故尧无对于天下，而许由与稷契为匹矣。何以言其然邪? 夫与物冥者，故群物之所不能离也。是以无心玄应，唯感之从，泛乎若不系之舟，东西之非己也。故无行而不与百姓共

who is always with the people no matter what he does is the ruler of the world wherever he may be.[1,2]

When a thousand people gather together without a person as their leader, they will be either disorderly or disorganized. Therefore when there are many virtuous people, there should not be many rulers, but when there is no virtuous person, there should be a ruler. This is the Way of Heaven and the most proper tiling to do.[3]

To cry as people cry is a manifestation of the mundane world. To identify life and death, forget joy and sorrow, and be able to sing in the presence of the corpse is the perfection of the transcendental world. ... Therefore principle has its ultimate, and the transcendental and the mundane world are in silent harmony with each other. There has never been a person who has roamed over the transcendental world to the utmost and yet was not silently in harmony with the mundane world, nor has there been anyone who was silently in harmony with the mundane world and yet did not roam over the transcendental world. Therefore the sage always roams in the transcendental world in order to enlarge the mundane world. By having no deliberate mind of his own, he is in accord with things.[4,5]

者，亦无往而不为天下之君矣。

千人聚，不以一人为主，不散则乱。故多贤不可以多君，无贤不可以无君。此天人之道，必至之宜。

人哭亦哭，俗内之迹也。齐死生，忘哀乐，临尸能歌，方外之至也。……夫理有至极，外内相冥，未有极游外之致而不冥于内者也，未有能冥于内而不游于外者也。故圣人常游外以宏内，无心以顺有……

---

1. Excerpted from Guo Xiang's comments on "Chapter One: Free And Easy Wandering" of *Zhuangzi*.
2. Comment from the translator: Practically all commentators praise or defend their authors. Guo Xiang, on the contrary, criticized Laozi and Zhuangzi. Like Wang Pi, he inclined to Daoism in his metaphysics but adhered to Confucianism in social and political philosophy. For this reason, he rated Confucius far above these Daoist philosophers.
3. Excerpted from Guo Xiang's comments on "Chapter Four: In the World of Men" of *Zhuangzi*.
4. Excerpted from Guo Xiang's comments on "Chapter Six: The Great and Venerable Teacher" of *Zhuangzi*.
5. Comment from the translator: As pointed out before, neither Wang Pi nor Guo Xiang considered Laozi or Zhuangzi a sage. Instead, their sage was Confucius. This is amazing, but the reason is really not far to seek. For to Guo Xiang, especially, the ideal person is a sage who is "sagely within and kingly without" and who travels in both the transcendental and mundane worlds. According to the Neo-Daoists, Laozi and Zhuangzi traveled only in the transcendental world and were therefore onesided, whereas Confucius was truly sagely within and kingly without.

The expert driver utilizes the natural capacity of horses to its limit. To use the capacity to its limit lies in letting it take its own course. If forced to run in rapid pace, with the expectation that they can exceed their capacity, horses will be unable to bear and many will die. On the other hand, if both worn-out and thoroughbred horses are allowed to use their proper strength and to adapt their pace to their given lot, even if they travel to the borders of the country, their nature will be fully preserved.

But there are those who, upon hearing the doctrine of allowing the nature of horses to take its own course, will say, "Then set the horses free and do not ride on them," and there are those who, upon hearing the doctrine of taking no action, will immediately say, "It is better to lie down than to walk." Why are they so much off the track and unable to return? In this they have missed Zhuangzi's ideas to a very high degree.[1]

夫善御者，将以尽其能也。尽能在于自任，而乃走作驰步，求其过能之用，故有不堪而多死焉。若乃任驽骥之力，适迟疾之分，虽则足迹接乎八荒之表，而众马之性全矣。

而惑者闻任马之性，乃谓放而不乘；闻无为之风，遂云行不如卧；何其往而不返哉！斯失乎庄生之旨远矣。

---

1. Excerpted from Guo Xiang's comments on "Chapter Nine: Horses' Hoofs" of *Zhuangzi*.

Extensive Reading C

The Perfection of the Chinese in the Art of Gardening[1]

Oliver Goldsmith

The English have not yet brought the art of gardening the same perfection with the Chinese, but have lately begun to imitate them; Nature is now followed with greater assiduity than formerly; the trees are suffered to shoot out the utmost luxuriance; the streams no longer forced from their native beds, are permitted to wind along the vallies; spontaneous flowers take place of the finished parterre, and the enameled meadow of the shaven green.

Yet still the English are far behind us in this charming art; their designers have not yet attained a power of uniting instruction with beauty. A European will scarcely conceive my meaning, when I say that there is scarce a garden in China which does not contain some fine moral, couched under the general design, where one is not taught wisdom as he walks, and feels the force of some noble truth or delicate precept resulting from the disposition of the groves, streams or grottoes. Permit me to illustrate what I mean by a description of my gardens at Quamsi. My heart still hovers round those scenes of former happiness with pleasure; and I find a satisfaction in enjoying them at this distance, though but in imagination.

You descended from the house between two groves of trees, planted in such a manner, that they were impenetrable to the eye; while on each hand the way was adorned with all that was beautiful in porcelain, statuary, and painting. This passage from the house opened into an area surrounded with rocks, flowers, trees, and shrubs, but all so disposed as if each was the spontaneous production of Nature. As you proceeded forward on this lawn, to your right and left hand were two gates, opposite each other, of very different architecture and design; and before you lay a temple built rather with minute elegance than ostentation.

The right hand gate was planned with the utmost simplicity, or rather rudeness; ivy clasped round the pillars, the baleful cypress hung over it; time seemed to have destroyed all the smoothness and regularity of the stone: two champions with lifted clubs appeared in the act of guarding its access; dragons and serpents were

---

1. Oliver Goldsmith, *The Citizen of the World*, London: J.M. Dent&Sons Ltd, 1934.

seen in the most hideous attitudes, to deter the spectator from approaching; and the perspective view that lay behind, seemed dark and gloomy to the last degree; the stranger was tempted to enter only from the motto: PERVIA VIRTUTI[1].

The opposite gate was formed in a very different manner; the architecture was light, elegant, and inviting; flowers hung in wreaths round the pillars; all was finished in the most exact and masterly manner; the very stone of which it was built, still preserved its polish; nymphs, wrought by the hand of a master in the most alluring attitudes, beckoned the stranger to approach; while all that lay behind, as far as the eye could reach, seemed gay and capable of affording endless pleasure. The motto itself contributed to invite him; for over the gate written these words FACILIS DESCENSUS[2].

By this time I fancy you begin to perceive that gloomy gate was designed to represent the road to Virtue; the opposite, the more agreeable passage to Vice. It is but natural to suppose, that the spectator was always to tempted to enter by the gate, which offered him so many allurement; I always in these cases left him to his choice; but generally found that he took to the left, which promised most entertainment.

Immediately upon his entering the gate of Vice, the trees and flowers were disposed in such a manner as to make the most pleasing impression; but as he walked farther on, he insensibly found the garden assume the air of a wilderness, the landscapes began to darken, the paths grew more intricate, he appeared to go downwards, frightful rocks seemed to hang over his head, gloomy caverns, unexpected precipices, awful ruins, heaps of unburied bones, and terrifying sounds, caused by unseen waters began to take place of what at first appeared so lovely; it was in vain to attempt returning, the labyrinth was too much perplexed for any but myself to find the way back. In short when sufficiently impressed with the horrors of what he saw, and the imprudence of his choice, I brought him by a hidden door, a shorter way back into the area from whence at first he had strayed.

The gloomy gate now presented itself before the stranger; and though there seemed little in its appearance to tempt his curiosity, yet encouraged by the motto, he generally proceeded. The darkness of the entrance, the frightful figures that seemed to obstruct his way, the trees of a mournful green, conspired at first to disgust him: as he went forward, however all began to open and wear a more pleasing appearance, beautiful cascades, beds of flowers, trees loaded with fruit or blossoms, and unexpected brooks, improved the scene: he now found that he was ascending, and, as he proceeded, all Nature grew more beautiful, the prospect

---

1. Latin, meaning "the Thoroughfare of Virtue."
2. Latin, meaning "The Path to Hell."

widened as he went higher, even the air itself, seemed to become more pure. Thus pleased and happy from unexpected beauties, I at last led him to an arbor, from whence he could view the garden, and the whole country around, and where he might own that the road to Virtue terminated in Happiness.

Though from this description you may imagine, that a vast tract of ground was necessary to exhibit such a pleasing variety in, yet be assured I have seen several gardens in England take up ten times the space which mine did, without half the beauty. A very small extent of ground is enough for an elegant taste; the greater room is required if magnificence is in view. There is no spot, though ever so little, which a skillful designer might not thus improve, so as to convey a delicate allegory, and impress the mind with truths the most useful and necessary. Adieu.

Extensive Reading D

Painting and Calligraphy from
The Heritage of Chinese Art [1]

Michael Sullivan

In China, painting, and more especially landscape-painting, is mistress of the arts. That this should be so seems not unnatural when we consider that one of the aims of Chinese philosophy and religion has always been to discover the workings of the universe and to attune man's actions to them. A Chinese painting, therefore, not only embodies the visible forms and forces of nature, but also displays the painter's understanding of their operation. His purpose is to present the subtle and complex forces of nature as harmoniously interacting, to show man in his true relationship to her, and to convey the life that is in all things by means of the springing vitality of his brushwork. In a sense, therefore, every picture, however slight, is a generalized philosophical, or rather metaphysical statement, even though it may be inspired by a particular place or memory. For the painter is not concerned with individual events, or with the accidents of time and place.

This generalization, this apparent detachment, so different from the passionate attachment to visible objects that we find in Rembrandt, Chardin, or Van Gogh—makes it difficult for the Western viewer to appreciate Chinese painting at first encounter. He finds it remote, tranquil, or merely decorative, and he is sometimes wearied in the long run by what he takes to be a sameness in style and content. The English critic Eric Newton, for example, finds Chinese painting, for all its charm, ultimately cold and unsatisfying; In its tendency to generalization he sees "an air of finality," that precludes any possibility of change, or development, or surprise. [2] There is some justification for this view. The restless "search for form," the experiments with style and technique which give such interest to the study of Western art, play little part in Chinese painting. Like the concert pianist, the Chinese painter must be fully a master of his technique and repertoire before he can consider presenting his work to others. He will not hesitate to make use of the vocabulary of "type-forms" and brush-strokes evolved by his predecessors; and

---

1. Raymond Dawson, *The Legacy of China*, Oxford: Clarendon Press, pp. 193–200.
2. *European Painting and Sculpture*, Harmondsworth, 1941, p. 30.

often it is only a highly trained eye that can detect the differences between two painters in the same tradition; between, say, figure studies by Qiu Ying and Tang Yin, or a landscape by Wen Zhengming and his nephew Wen Boren. And yet, in another sense, the Chinese painter's statement is anything but final; for only a clear statement about something specific can be final—Chardin's bottles, for example, or a Rembrandt self-portrait. On the contrary, he is acutely aware that he is only hinting at the truth; whether he presents a swiftly sketched spray of bamboo, or a vast panorama of mountains and valleys, he is giving us no more than a glimpse of a totality that lies beyond expression.

The apparent lack of perspective in Chinese painting is bound up with this desire to avoid a complete or finite statement. If by perspective we mean the delineation of forms on a flat surface as they would appear to a viewer standing at a fixed point, then Chinese painting indeed has no perspective. The eleventh-century critic Shen Kuo took the landscapist Li Cheng to task for his skill in what he called "painting his eaves from below." "This is absurd," he wrote. "All landscapes have to be viewed from the angle of totality to behold the part.... If we apply his method to the painting of mountains, we are unable to see more than one layer of the mountain at one time. How could we then see the totality of its unending ranges?... Li Cheng surely does not understand the principle of viewing the part from the angle of totality. His measurement of height and distance is certainly a fine thing. But should one attach paramount importance to the angles and corners of buildings?" Shen Kuo objects to Li Cheng's application of the principle of onepoint perspective because it sets arbitrary limits to the power of the artist to embrace the whole. There are indications that until the end of the Northern Song Dynasty at least, other painters beside Li Cheng were making experiments along these lines, a remarkable example being the long hand-scroll by Zhang Zeduan depicting preparations for the Qingming festival which has recently been discovered in China. But such experiments ceased after the end of Northern Song, when the aim of the scholar-painter was no longer to reveal nature but to express himself. Most characteristic of Chinese landscape-painting in all periods is what might be termed a continuous perspective, which shifts horizontally in the hand-scroll and vertically in the hanging scroll, so that the view of each successive area is correct to the eye directly opposite that point. By thus avoiding a fixed viewpoint, and by the subtle placing in his panorama of a winding mountain path, a ferry, perhaps a tea-house, and a few small figures, the painter not only creates the illusion of an actual landscape, but he also cunningly invites us to explore it.

The Chinese view of what constitutes suitable subject-matter for painting presents another striking contrast with that of Europe. The Chinese painter's aim is always to present a view of the world that is satisfying and spiritually refreshing;

consequently only themes which carry this message would he consider worthy of his brush. He would regard with horror the rapes, executions, and massacres which, whether of religious inspiration or not, we are trained to contemplate as works of art; for to him art is indivisible, and our Western ability to admire color, form, and composition in a picture without being in any way affected by distasteful subjectmatter implies, if not a corrupt view of the world, then at least a dangerously fragmented one.

The lofty calm and detachment from worldly things implicit in a Chinese painting suggests that the painter himself lived in a world apart. But this was only partly true. While some of China's greatest painters—Ni Zan, for example, or Shi Qi—have been eccentrics and hermits, many led an active public life, whether as cabinet minister or district magistrate, which brought them face to face with the world and its problems. But when these men returned home at the end of a busy day to paint a landscape or compose verses, they deliberately left the "dusty world" behind them. The Ming scholar-painter Wen Zhengming, for example, was during the middle years of his life too busy with his historical work in the Hanlin Academy to spend his time wandering in the mountains, as he no doubt would have preferred. But he could still take up his brush to paint a landscape panorama that would bring refreshment to himself and pleasure to his friends. To say that such a painting was "escapist" might suggest that it was insincere. Yet it was a in the highest sense escapist because it liberated the mind from material things. To achieve this, a painting had to be tranquil, harmonious, and meaningful. Mere originality counted for little or nothing.[1]

To fulfill its role, moreover, it was necessary that a painting conform in its colors and shapes to those of nature, not because realism as such was desirable, but because not to paint things correctly would suggest that the artist did not understand them. Accuracy in depicting the procession of the seasons, for example, with the trees and plants in their appropriate colors and foliage was an outward sign of a deeper understanding. But accuracy alone was never enough. Too meticulous a conformity to nature would rob the painting of the quality essential above all—vitality; for it was through the springing movement of the artist's (and the calligrapher's) brush that he expressed his awareness of the life of nature. Finally, and increasingly as time went on, it was desirable that the painting should contain some reference, in composition or brushwork, or even merely in title, to the work

---

1. An excellent introduction to Chinese painting from the Chinese point of view is Chiang Yee, *The Chinese Eye* (London, 1935). Other works include William Cohn, *Chinese Painting* (London, 1957); Sherman E. Lee, *Chinese Landscape Painting* (revised edition, Cleveland, 1962); while James Cahill's *Chinese Painting* (Geneva, 1960) is notable for its fresh outlook and sympathetic treatment of the literary school, Siren's *Chinese Painting* (7 vols., London, 1956 and 1958) is encyclopedic in its scope.

of some great master of the past.

These fundamental requirements of a painting were, so far as we know, first set down in writing by the painter and critic Xie He (5th century) in the short preface to his classified list of still earlier masters. His celebrated "six principles" might be briefly translated as follows: spiritconsonance and life-movement; the "bone method" in the use of the brush; conformity to the shapes of objects in nature; conformity to their colors; care in placing and arranging the elements in the composition; transmission of the tradition by copying past models. Fidelity to nature and convincing scale relationships were particularly important during this formative period, when painters were still wrestling with elementary problems of proportion and distance; while the last principle enshrines an attitude to tradition which is unique to China, and is discussed further in the next section of this chapter. Later critics and theorists emphasized one aspect or another, but all were agreed upon the fundamental importance of the first. Xie He's Qi Yun ("spiritconsonance"). Its precise meaning has been endlessly debated, and every Western historian of Chinese art has produced his own rendering of the term. It may simply be said that it concerns the vital cosmic spirit or breath (Qi) to which the painter must attune himself (yun) if he is to be able to express the life and movement, or perhaps life-in-movement, that is manifest in nature. This vitality is conveyed by means of the second principle, the structural strength and tension of the brush-stroke, implied by the apt use of the "bone" image, that painting and calligraphy share incommon.[1]

It was through the practice of calligraphy—whether the square, powerful li-shu (clerk's hand) of the Han Dynasty, the elegant standard kai-shu, the cursive xing-shu, or the still more cursive cao-shu (grass writing)—that the scholar-gentleman refined and developed his sense of balance, movement, and form[2]. Calligraphy has often been compared to modern Western abstract expressionism and "action painting," for both are the product of the controlled nervous energy of the hand that holds the brush. But the comparison is a misleading one. For the Western abstract painter, pure form, divorced from content, is all; form, in fact, is content. But even the most extreme of Chinese expressionists always sought a meaning beyond pure form. The passage of calligraphy would be less admirable if it were totally illegible or its content trivial. In painting, the most outrageous techniques of the modern abstract expressionists were anticipated by Chinese eccentrics in

---

1. Osvald Sirén's *Chinese on the Art of Painting* (Peking, 1936), of which a revised edition is in preparation, provides a useful introduction to Chinese critical and theoretical writings, some of which are translated and discussed in more detail in William R. B. Acker, *Some Tang and Pre-Tang Texts on Chinese Painting* (Leiden, 1954).
2. Chiang Yee, *Chinese Calligraphy* (London, 1954), is a good general introduction to this subject.

the eighth and ninth centuries: one master would flip his ink-soaked hair at the silk; another splash it with ink while he danced to music, facing in the opposite direction; a third would spread ink in pools on silk laid out on the floor, then drag an assistant round and round sitting on a sheet. But these bizarre methods were never ends in themselves. The records tell us—for unhappily not one of these remarkable pictures has survived—that having thus spilled their ink, the painters then proceeded, by the deft addition of scattered trees, waterfalls, and pavilions, to turn their smears and blotches into landscapes. The Zen ink painters of the twelfth and thirteenth centuries expressed their moment of illumination in brushwork hardly less explosive. Here at least we might expect to find pure abstraction. But Mu Xi and Ying Yuqian conveyed their metaphysical excitement not in empty gestures with the brush, but in the shape of a monk tearing up the sutras, or a mountain village emerging out of the mist. For the painter, as for the calligrapher, mere form was never enough.

Extensive Reading E

A Selection from *The Tao and the Logos* [1]

Zhang Longxi

The Ironic Pattern

It seems an inevitable irony that the philosopher always has to say a good deal about what he believes to be ineffable and to write a good deal to elucidate what is supposedly absent in writing. Instead of being silent, Wittgenstein writes about the inexpressible in epigrammatic propositions which he acknowledges to be ultimately senseless (*unsinnig*) and which he urges the reader to throw away once he has understood them. Similarly Laozi composes a book of five thousand characters to speak of the tao that cannot be tao-ed (spoken of), and Zhuangzi tries to demonstrate the ineffable in a dazzling display of metaphors, parables, and images, while searching for the man who will forget his words once he has got the meaning. The loophole or exit Russell mentions turns out to be nothing but speaking and writing, something these philosophers did not mean to use but ended up using profusely. They all have to say that they mean to be silent, and they all have to write to declare that they do not trust writing. Yet nothing abides but writing; even the debasement of writing. Philosophers' anxiety over writing begins with their misgivings concerning the discrepancy between thoughts and words, especially words used figuratively, but in the end they all use words, and use them in all kinds of rhetorical ways. The dream of a univocal language without any figure or metaphor, as Derrida says, remains a "dream at the heart of philosophy."[2] Derrida attempts to expose the emptiness of this dream, the philosopher's futile search for a language of unmediated presence, by quoting Anatole France that "the very metaphysicians who think to escape. The world of appearances are constrained to live perpetually in allegory. A sorry lot of poets, they dim the colors of the ancient fables, and are themselves but gatherers of fables. They produce white mythology."[3]

---

1. Excerpted from Zhang, Longxi, "Philosopher, Mystic, Poet," *The Tao and the Logos—Literary Hermeneutics: East and West*, Durham & London: Duke University Press, 1992. p. 38.
2. Derrida, "White Mythology," *Margins of Philosophy*, p. 268.
3. Anatole France, *The Garden of Epicurus* (Alfred Allinson trans.), quoted in Derrida, *Margins of Philosophy*, p. 213.

Indeed, in using images and analogies, philosophical discourse at times verges on the intense metaphoricity of poetry. Kant points out the inescapable figurative nature of all philosophical expressions when he observe that language is replete with indirect exhibitions which "express concepts not by means of a direct intuition but only according to an analogy with one, i.e. a transfer of our reflection on an object of intuition to an entirely different concept, to which perhaps no intuition can ever directly correspond."[1] He sees dearly that the inescapable metaphoricity of language constitutes the very substance of philosophical discourse, and puts the distinction between philosophical and poetic expressions its question. An examination of the language philosophers use can bear this out. The epigrammatic form of Wittgenstein's writing has a touch of wit and raciness reminiscent of many of Schiller's aphorisms or Novalis's fragments. In turning out numerous metaphors in quick succession, Zhuangzi, as he himself describes, uses words like wine goblets to be filled or emptied as the occasion requires, achieving a highly literary kind of writing that is richly packed with "airy and fantastic sayings, absurd and bombastic phrases, and words without ends or boundaries."[2] Even Plato, who accuses poets of lying and banishes them from his ideal state, expounds the Socratic philosophy in the form of dialogues which Aristotle classifies as a literary genre "between poetry and prose."[3] In many ways Aristotle's Poetics is a defense of poetry against Plato's rationalistic attack, and ever since the Renaissance many apologists of poetry have claimed that Plato himself is a poet, for "whoever well considereth shall find," as Sir Philip Sidney contends, "that in the body of his work, though the inside and strength were philosophy, the skin as it were and beauty depended most of poetry."[4] In much the same vein, Shelley also claims that "Plato was essentially a poet," for "the truth and splendor of his imagery, and the melody of his language, is the most intense that it is possible to conceive."[5]

If Sidney still locates the metaphoricity of Plato's writing in the frame of an inner/outer dichotomy, considering it as the mere outside, long before him Dante already realizes that metaphor is more than just embedded in the texture of philosophical discourse but may be said to constitute the very philosophical discourse itself. In his well-known "Letter to Can Grande," Dante argues that it is metaphor that enables the philosopher to express thoughts that otherwise may remain silent and inexpressible: "For we see many things with the intellect for which

---

1. Kant, *Critique of Judgment*, sec.59, p. 228.
2. *Zhuangzi*, xxxiii, p. 474.
3. Aristotle, On Poets 2, *Poetics*, p. 56.
4. Sir Philip Sidney, *An Apology for Poetry*, Indianapolis: Bobbs-Merrill,1970, p. 8.
5. Percy Bysshe Shelley, "A Defense of Poetry," *Shelley's Critical Prose*, Lincoln: University of Nebraska Press, 1967, p. 9.

there are no verbal signs. This fact Plato makes plain enough by the use he makes of metaphors in his books: for he see many things by the light of the intellect which he was unable to express in appropriate words."[1] Therefore it is through images, metaphors, analogies, and other figures of speech that philosophical conceptions take graspable shape and become intelligible. We can almost say that metaphor, in philosophy as well as in poetry, "gives to aery nothing/A local habitation and a name."[2] The unnamed is inconceivable, and philosophy as such exists only in words and names. Despite Zhuangzi's advice to forget the word, it is ironically his words that have made him best remembered, for many people read Zhuangzi as one of the greatest prose writers in classical Chinese literature: they admire the grandeur of his imagination and the beauty of his language, even though they do not care about his Daoist ideology. That is to say, people tend to remember his words while forgetting his meaning, and Zhuangzi's advice functions against itself as a poetic trope, an irony. And his philosophy of self-effacement, like that of Laozi, is thus overturned by his own writing.

Zhuangzi's highly figurative text shows clearly how the play of metaphor blurs the usual distinction between philosophy and literature. In his particular case, however, the mythology emerging from the text is by no means white, but of a very robust and sanguine color. Neither is Zhuangzi unaware of the irreducible metaphoricity of his writing, but he would take it as an unfortunate necessity. Hui Shi, a rival philosopher, challenges Zhuangzi that he does, after all, use many words despite his protest that words are quite useless. In response to that challenge, Zhuangzi answers wittily in a typical irony: "But you must know they are useless, and then you can talk about their use." He seems to argue that once you know that the use of words is provisional, you are freed, as it were, from the infatuation with words and are thus capable of using words as expedient "non-words." "Speaking those non-words," Zhuangzi argues, "you may talk all your life without having said anything. Otherwise, even if you never speak in all your life, you may still have said too much."[3] So the issue at stake is not so much speaking itself as the right kind of medium one uses in speaking. By using words as "non-words," Zhuangzi carries out a double-edged argument, for on the one hand, language becomes for him a mere instrument to convey meaning, like the trap for catching fish or the snare to get the hare: a disposable instrument once its purpose is served; while on the other hand, the philosopher has the excuse to use language any way he pleases to convey the meaning, including using all sorts of

---

1. Dante Alighieri, *Literary Criticism of Dante Alighieri*, (R.S. Haller trans.), Lincoln: University of Nebraska Press, 1973, p. 110.
2. William Shakespeare, *A Midnight Summer's Dream*, 5.1.16, Boston: Houghton Mifflin, 1974.
3. *Zhuangzi*, xxxvi, p. 403; xxxvii, p. 409.

rhetorical devices and maneuvers. But what exactly are Zhuangzi's "non-words"? What else, if not the irreducible metaphors necessary for bringing the unnamed and the unnameable into existence, metaphors the philosophers has to smuggle back into his writing after he has denied their usefulness? When Zhuangzi called for the man who would forget his words while preserving his meaning, he seemed to know that he was never to find such a man. We may also recall that Confucius, despite his wish to be silent, nevertheless acknowledges the necessity of speaking to transmit what the sages have already said in the past. Much as they would desire a transparent and wordless transmission of truth and knowledge, philosophers, no less than the poets, thus find themselves deeply immersed in language and its inescapable metaphoricity. Apparently, the desire for silence will find catharsis in an ironic pattern, for the more one craves silence, the more desperately one must speak and write. To some extent, Richard Rorty argues that it is recognition of this ironic pattern that differentiates deconstruction from traditional philosophy. "Philosophical writing, for Heidegger as for the Kantians," he puts it summarily, "is really aimed at putting an end to writing. For Derrida, writing always leads to more writing, and more, and still more."[1] Perhaps we may say that Zhuangzi, by using words as "non-words," also recognized this ironic pattern, offering philosophers an excuse to recuperate writing, a license to proliferate writing even to infinity, because Zhuangzi's use of "non words" can be understood as essentially a move to reclaim language and to acknowledge the inevitable metaphorcity of all philosophical discourse.

---

1. Rorty, "Philosophy as A Kind of Writing: An Essay on Derrida," *New Literary History* 10 (August 1978): p. 145.

Study Questions

1. Which statements in the Excerpts from *Dao De Jing* are reflective of the Daoist philosophy of movement in reverse? How does it relate to the idea of movement in *The Book of Changes*?

2. The working of the Five Agents is also mentioned in "The External" from *Zhuangzi*. Does it remind you of any Neo-Confucian work? If it does, please make a comparison between the two descriptions of them.

3. Which allusions in "The External" are to infer to Confucian ideas? How are they integrated within the writing of the prose? How do they inform you of Zhuangzi's style of writing?

4. When we compare Laozi and Zhuangzi, we may find that the former is a more sophisticated verse-writer, yet the latter is a more humorous prose-writer. Besides this difference, can you find other contrasts to be made between the two Daoist philosophers?

5. What does the story of Butcher Ding tell us about Zhuangzi's attitude toward knowledge, training of skills and the benefits of skills/knowledge? Does the story advise us to give up knowing or to know for living in a more skillful way? Do you think Zhuangzi's ideas reflect a sort of Daoist anti-intellectualism?

6. In *Intellectual Foundations of China*, Frederick W. Mote states that to philosophical Daoists, the highest ideal is "the acceptance of Nature." The inclination to return to Nature is also found in Romanticism, the intellectual and literary movement that occurred in Europe toward the end of the 18th century. Here excerpted are lines that described the development from the primitive status of human beings to the civilized status from *A Discourse upon the Origin and the Foundation of the Inequality Among Mankind* by the important French Philosopher Jean Jacques Rousseau, whose thoughts led to Pre-Romanticism. List the contrasted points of the two kinds of "nature," and then consider how they help you further your understanding of Daoism?

    Let us conclude that savage man, wandering about in the forests, without industry, without speech, without any fixed residence, an equal stranger to war and every social connection, without standing in any shape in need of his fellows, as well as without any desire of hurting them, and perhaps even without ever distinguishing them individually one from the other, subject to few passions, and finding in himself all he wants, let us, I say, conclude that savage man thus circumstanced had no knowledge or sentiment but such as are proper to that condition, that he was alone sensible of his real necessities, took notice of nothing but what it was his interest to see, and that his understanding made as little progress as his vanity. If he happened to make any discovery, he could the less communicate it as he did not even know his children. The art perished with the inventor; there was neither education nor improvement; generations succeeded generations to no purpose; and as all constantly set out from the same point, whole centuries rolled on in the rudeness and barbarity of the first age; the species was grown old, while the individual still remained in a state of childhood.

...

Behold then all our faculties developed; our memory and imagination at work, self-love interested; reason rendered active; and the mind almost arrived at the utmost bounds of that perfection it is capable of. Behold all our natural qualities put in motion; the rank and condition of every man established, not only as to the quantum of property and the power of serving or hurting others, but likewise as to genius, beauty, strength or address, merit or talents; and as these were the only qualities which could command respect, it was found necessary to have or at least to affect them. It was requisite for men to be thought what they really were not. To be and to appear became two very different things, and from this distinction sprang pomp and knavery, and all the vices which form their train. On the other hand, man, heretofore free and independent, was now in consequence of a multitude of new wants brought under subjection, as it were, to all nature, and especially to his fellows, whose slave in some sense he became even by becoming their master; if rich, he stood in need of their services, if poor, of their assistance; even mediocrity itself could not enable him to do without them. He must therefore have been continually at work to interest them in his happiness, and make them, if not really, at least apparently find their advantage in laboring for his: this rendered him sly and artful in his dealings with some, imperious and cruel in his dealings with others, and laid him under the necessity of using ill all those whom he stood in need of, as often as he could not awe them into a compliance with his will, and did not find it his interest to purchase it at the expense of real services. In fine, an insatiable ambition, the rage of raising their relative fortunes, not so much through real necessity, as to over-top others, inspire all men with a wicked inclination to injure each other, and with a secret jealousy so much the more dangerous, as to carry its point with the greater security, it often puts on the face of benevolence. In a word, sometimes nothing was to be seen but a contention of endeavoring on the one hand, and an opposition of interests on the other, while a secret desire of thriving at the expense of others constantly prevailed. Such were the first effects of property, and the inseparable attendants of infant inequality.[1]

7. Read through Extensive Reading A, C, and D on Chinese traditional art. Figure out which features of Chinese traditional art forms reveal the Daoist imaginativeness.

---

1. Jean Jacques Rousseau, *A Discourse upon the Origin and the Foundation of the Inequality Among Mankind,* The Project Gutenberg EBook.

CHAPTER ❹

Chinese Buddhism

1. Ji Xianlin, the well-known Chinese Indologist, once said, "The river of Chinese civilization has kept alternating between rising and falling, but it has never dried up, because there was always fresh water flowing into it. It has over history been joined by fresh water many times, the two largest inflows coming from India and the West, both of which owed their success to translation. It is translation that has preserved the perpetual youth of Chinese civilization. Translation is hugely useful!" Recall some of the Chinese translations of Buddhist concepts that you have known, and look for their original Sanskrit versions.

2. There are scholars of Buddhism who believe that horse plays a fairly important role in Buddhism, as seen from the transmission of Buddhism into different cultures on horse backs, the equestrian-style clothes and apparatuses of early Buddhist missionaries. Please do more research on the pieces of evidence that either prove or disprove such a point.

Introduction

While we can't deny the Greek and Roman influence on Gandharan Buddhist art along with Greco-Bactrian invasions, we have to recognize the inflow of the equestrian culture that carried early Buddhist missionaries and scriptures from Kushan Empire to the sedentary agricultural society of China during the late Warring States period. Horse thus has become an icon closely related to Buddhist transmission, whose traces were not only to be found on the silk road that connected North China with Central and Western Asia, on the gold coins of Kushan Empire, from the changed dressing styles of soldiers as seen in their robes and boots in the Warring State of Zhao, but also in the white-horse legend that romanticized the very cause for which Ming Emperor in Eastern Han was to encourage the importing of the esoteric religion into China[1].

The early writings on Buddhism, with its blending of Buddhist and Chinese classical concepts, demonstrated a conspicuous attempt to integrate the foreign within the indigenous. Stylized in the dialectic discourse reminiscent of that of *The Analects of Confucius*, "The Disposition of Error," ascribed to Mou Rong in Eastern Han, made an effort to justify the equal status of Buddhist wisdom with that of the Chinese classics. Obviously in the above-mentioned text, the new philosophy needed to be credited by way of the classical philosophical and ethical frameworks of Confucianism and Daoism, hence we are not surprised to find the use of Dao to imply Buddhist dharma, the comparison of Buddha with the Chinese sages, the juxtaposition of Nirvana with Daoist transcendence, etc., in this piece of early writing on Chinese Buddhism. "The error" in the title is probably more revealing of the fact that Buddhism had brought onto itself a rather considerable popularity than that it had been devastatingly targeted against, since "the disposition" itself should have been unnecessary if Buddhism had not appealed strongly to a large number of Chinese people during that time.

The popularization of Buddhism among Chinese, as seen in its development, does not merely happen to a certain social stratum, but to all. Even though there have been times when Buddhism was suppressed by rulers, it has more often been a spiritual weapon, first and most conspicuously in North Wei Emperor Xiaowen's political and cultural agenda, while they sought to legitimate and solidify their ruling in central China. The religion's graphic accounts of the wheels of life and

---

1. Such a legend, while famous, has never been solidified by any historical evidence.

the status of enlightenment were so conveniently rendered into the Chinese imagination of the other worlds that it has become a natural element in Chinese folk culture; and the metaphysical contemplation and difficulty of translation involved in the transmission of Buddhist scriptures have made the religion most appealing to Chinese intellectuals and elites.

The development of Chinese Buddhism has also testified to the great capacity of Chinese culture in that it embraces what may be foreign in the first place and then makes it grow into its own genes. With the already highly developed Confucian and Daoist philosophy, Chinese elites turned to Buddhist scriptures to look for more to enrich their knowledge about both the metaphysical and physical worlds, which in turn helped to develop Neo-Daoism and Neo-Confucianism. Along the process, we find many features of Chinese Buddhism that can never be found either in its Indian origin or its other developed versions in other cultures. Despite its great diversity of schools, Chinese Buddhism has displayed a tendency to convey the abstruse through the tangible, to reach the emptiness through particular ways of being. From the text of *Confirmation of the Consciousness-Only System*, which represents the most subtle and abstract extreme of early Chinese rendition of Buddhism, to the *Platform Sutra*, which reflects the initial teaching of the Meditation School of Zen, as excerpted in this chapter, one could catch a glimpse of how the Chinese mind could turn a pure idealist sophistication of the universe into a much more immediate introspection of the "great insight" that can be readily practiced and achieved.

Selected Passages from
The Disposition of Error

《理惑论》选篇

Mouzi[1]

牟子

Why is Buddhism Not Mentioned in the Chinese Classics?

The questioner said: If the way of the Buddha is the greatest and most venerable of ways, why did Yao, Shun, the Duke of Zhou, and Confucius not practice it? In the seven Classics one sees no mention of it. You, sir, are fond of *The Book of Odes* and *The Book of History*, and you take pleasure in rites and music. Why, then, do you love the way of the Buddha and rejoice in outlandish arts? Can they exceed the Classics and commentaries and beautify the accomplishments of the sages? Permit me the liberty, sir, of advising you to reject them.

Mouzi said: All written works need not necessarily be the words of Confucius, and all medicine does not necessarily consist of the formulae of [the famous physician] Bian Que. What accords with principle is to be followed, what heals the sick is good. The gentleman-scholar draws widely on all forms of good, and thereby benefits his character. Zi Gong [a disciple of Confucius] said, "Did the Master have a permanent teacher?" Yao served Yin Shou, Shun served Wu Cheng, the Duke of Zhou learned from Lü Wang, and Confucius learned from Laozi. And none of these teachers is mentioned in the seven Classics. Although these four teachers were sages, to compare them to the Buddha would be like comparing a white deer to a unicorn, or a swallow to a phoenix. Yao, Shun, the Duke of Zhou, and Confucius learned even from such teachers as these. How much less, then, may one reject the Buddha, whose distinguishing marks are extraordinary and whose superhuman powers know no

问曰：佛道至尊至大。尧舜周孔曷不修之乎。七经之中不见其辞。子既耽诗书悦礼乐。奚为复好佛道喜异术。岂能踰经传美圣业哉。窃为吾子不取也。

牟子曰：书不必孔丘之言。药不必扁鹊之方。合义者从。愈病者良。君子博取众善以辅其身。子贡云。夫子何常师之有乎。尧事尹寿。舜事务成。且学吕望。丘学老聃。亦俱不见于七经也。四师虽圣。比之于佛。犹白鹿之与麒麟。燕鸟之与凤凰也。尧舜周孔。且犹与之。况佛身相好变化神力无方。焉能舍而不学乎。五经事义或有所阙。佛不见记何足怪疑哉。

---

1. Wm. Theodore de Bary, Wing-Tsit Chan, and Burton Watson, *Sources of Chinese Tradition*, New York: Columbia University Press.

bounds! How may one reject him and refuse to learn from him? The records and teachings of the Five Classics do not contain everything. Even if the Buddha is not mentioned in them, what occasion is there for suspicion?

Why Do Monks Not Marry?

The questioner said: Now of felicities there is none greater than the continuation of one's line, of unfilial conduct there is none worse than childlessness. The monks forsake wife and children, reject property and wealth. Some do not marry all their lives. How opposed this conduct is to felicity and filial piety! ...

问曰：夫福莫逾于继嗣。不孝莫过于无后。沙门弃妻子捐货财终身不娶。何违其福孝之行也。……

Mouzi said: ... Wives, children, and property are the luxuries of the world, but simple living and inaction are the wonders of the Way. Laozi has said, "Of reputation and life, which is dearer? Or life and property, which is worth more?"... Xu You and Chao Fu dwelt in a tree. Bo Yi and Shu Qi starved in Shouyang, but Confucius praised their worth, saying, "They sought to act in accordance with humanity and they succeeded in acting so." One does not hear of their being ill spoken of because they were childless and propertyless. The monk practices the way and substitutes that for the pleasures of disporting himself in the world He accumulates goodness and wisdom in exchange for the joys of wife and children.

牟子曰：……妻子财物世之余也。清躬无为道之妙也。老子曰。名与身孰亲。身与货孰多。……许由栖巢木。夷齐饿首阳。圣孔称其贤曰。求仁得仁者也。不闻讥其无后无货也。沙门修道德。以易游世之乐反淑贤以贷妻子之欢。

Death and Rebirth

The questioner said: The Buddhists say that after a man dies he will be reborn. I do not believe in the truth of these words.

问曰：佛道言。人死当复更生。仆不信此言之审也。

Mouzi said: ... The spirit never perishes. Only the body decays. The body is like the roots and leaves of the five grains, the spirit is like the seeds and kernels of the five grains. When the roots and leaves come forth they inevitably die. But do the seeds and kernels perish? Only the body of one who has achieved the Way perishes. ...

牟子曰：……魂神固不灭矣。但身自朽烂耳。身譬如五谷之根叶。魂神如五谷之种实。根叶生必当死。种实岂有终已。得道身灭耳。

Someone said: If one follows the Way one dies. If one does not follow the Way one dies. What difference is there?

或曰：为道亦死。不为道亦死。有以异

Mouzi said: You are the sort of person who, having not a single day of goodness, yet seeks a lifetime of fame. If one has the Way, even if one dies one's soul goes to an abode of happiness. If one does not have the Way, when one is dead one's soul suffers misfortune.

Why Should A Chinese Allow Himself to Be Influenced by Indian Ways?

The questioner said: Confucius said, "The barbarians with a ruler are not so good as the Chinese without one." Mencius criticized Chen Xiang for rejecting his own education to adopt the ways of [the teacher of agricultural science] Xu Xing, saying, "I have heard of using what is Chinese to change what is barbarian, but I have never heard of using what is barbarian to change what is Chinese." You, sir, at the age of twenty learned the way of Yao, Shun, Confucius, and the Duke of Zhou. But now you have rejected them, and instead have taken up the arts of the barbarians. Is this not a great error?

Mouzi said: ... What Confucius said was meant to rectify the way of the world, and what Mencius was meant to deplore onesidedness. Of old, when Confucius was thinking of taking residence among the nine barbarian nations, he said, "If a gentleman-scholar dwells in their midst, what baseness can there be among them?" ...

The Commentary says, "The north polar star is in the center of heaven and to the north of man." From this one can see that the land of China is not necessarily situated under the center of heaven. According to the Buddhist scriptures, above, below, and all around, all beings containing blood belong to the Buddha-clan.

Therefore I revere and study these scriptures. Why should I reject the Way of Yao, Shun, Confucius, and the Duke of Zhou? Gold and jade do not harm each other, crystal and amber do not cheapen each other. You say that another is in error when it is you yourself who err.

乎。

牟子曰：所谓无一日之善。而问终身之誉者也。有道虽死神归福堂。为恶既死神当其殃。

问曰:孔子曰。夷狄之有君。不如诸夏之亡也。孟子讥陈相更学许行之术曰。吾闻用夏变夷。未闻夷变夏者也。吾子弱冠学尧舜周孔之道。而今舍之更学夷狄之术。不已惑乎。

牟子曰：……孔子所言矫世法矣。孟轲所云疾专一耳。昔孔子欲居九夷。曰君子居之。何陋之有。……

传曰：北辰之星。在天之中。在人之北。以此观之。汉地未必为天中也。佛经所说上下周极。含血之类物皆属佛焉。

是以吾复尊而学之。何为当舍尧舜周孔之道。金玉不相伤。隋璧不相妨。谓人为惑。特自惑乎。

Selected Passages from *Confirmation of the Consciousness-Only System Translated from Sanskrit*

《成唯识论》
选篇

Xuan zang[1]

玄奘 译

The verse [by Vasubandhu] says:

First of all, the storehouse [ālaya] consciousness, which brings into fruition the seeds [effects of good and evil seeds].

[In its state of pure consciousness] it is not conscious of its clinging and impressions. In both its objective and subjective functions it is always associated with touch, volition, feeling, sensation, thought, and cognition. But it is always indifferent to its associations.

The Treatise says:

The first transformation of consciousness is called ālaya in both the Mahāyāna and Hīnayāna. ... Why are the seeds so-called? It means that in consciousness itself fruitions, functions, and differentiations spontaneously arise. These are neither the same nor different from the consciousness or from what they produce....

In this way the other consciousnesses which "perfume" [affect] it and the consciousness which is perfumed arises and perishes together, and the concept of perfuming is thus established. To enable the seeds that lie within what is perfumed [storehouse consciousness] to grow, as the hemp plant is perfumed, is called perfuming. As soon as the seeds are produced, the consciousnesses which can perfume become in their turn causes which perfume and produce seeds. The three dharmas [the seeds, the manifestations, and perfuming] turn on and on, simultaneously acting as cause and effect....

颂曰：
初阿赖耶识，

异熟一切种，不可知执受，处了常与触、作意、受、想、思，相应唯舍受。

论曰：
初能变识大小乘教名阿赖耶。……此中何法名为种子。谓本识中亲生自果功能差别。此与本识及所生果不一不异。……

如是能熏与所熏识俱生俱灭熏习义成。

令所熏中种子生长如熏苣蕂故名熏习。能熏识等从种生时。即能为因复熏成种。

三法展转因果同时。

---

1. Wm. Theodore de Bary, Wing-Tsit Chan, and Burton Watson, *Sources of Chinese Tradition*, New York: Columbia University Press, 1960, p. 306.

The verse says:

Based on the root-consciousness [ālaya], the five consciousnesses [of the senses] manifest themselves in accordance with the conditioning factors. Sometimes [the senses manifest themselves] together and sometimes not, just as waves [manifest themselves] depending on water conditions. The sense-center consciousness always arises and manifests itself, except when born in the realm of the absence of thought, in the state of unconsciousness, in the two forms of concentration, in sleep, and in that state where the spirit is depressed or absent.

The Treatise says:

The root consciousness is the storehouse consciousness because it is the root from which all pure and impure consciousnesses grow. ... By "conditioning factors" are meant the mental activities, the sense organs, and sense objects. It means that the five consciousnesses are dependent internally upon the root consciousness and externally follow the combination of the conditions of the mental activities, the five sense organs, and sense objects. They [the senses] manifest themselves together and sometimes separately. This is so because the external conditions may come to be combined suddenly or gradually.

The verse says:

Thus the various consciousnesses are but transformations. That which discriminates and that which is discriminated are, because of this, both unreal. For this reason, everything is mind only.

The Treatise says:

The various consciousnesses refer to the three transformations of consciousness previously discussed and their mental qualities. They are all capable of transforming into two seeming portions, the perceiving portion and the perceived portion. The term "transformation" is thus employed. The perceiving portion that has been transformed is called "discrimination" because it can apprehend the perceived portion [as the object of perception]. The perceived portion that has been

颂曰：

依止根本识，
五识随缘现，
或俱或不俱，
如涛波依水，
意识常现起，
除生无想天，
及无心二定，
睡眠与闷绝。

论曰：

根本识者阿赖耶识。染净诸识生根本故。……缘谓作意根境等缘。谓五识身内依本识。外随作意五根境等众缘和合方得现前。

由此或俱或不俱起。外缘合者有顿渐故。

颂曰：

是诸识转变，分别所分别，由此彼皆无，故一切唯识。

论曰：

是诸识者。谓前所说三能变识及彼心所。皆能变似见相二分。

立转变名。
所变见分说名分别，
能取相故。
所变相分名所分别，

113

transformed is called the "object of discrimination" because it is apprehended by the perceiving portion. According to this correct principle, aside from what is transformed in consciousness, the self and dharmas[1] are both definitely nonexistent, because apart from what apprehends and what is apprehended, there is nothing else, and because there are no real things apart from the two portions.

见所取故。
由此正理彼实我法离识
所变皆定非有。
离能所取无别物故。
非有实物离二相故。

Therefore everything created [by conditions] and non-created, everything seemingly real or unreal, is all inseparable from consciousness.

是故一切有为无为
若实若假皆不离识。

---

1. In Buddhism, dharma means "cosmic law and order," but is also applied to the teachings of the Buddha. In Buddhist philosophy, dhamma/dharma is also the term for "phenomena."

An Excerpt from *A Record of Buddhist Monasteries in Luoyang*[1]

《洛阳伽蓝记》
选篇

The Baode temple (Temple of Repayment of virtue) was established by Emperor Xiaowen, [otherwise known as] Gaozu, and dedicated to his grandmother Empress Feng[2] for her posthumous happiness. It was located three li outside the Kaiyang Gate and to the east of the Imperial Drive.

报德寺，高祖孝文皇帝所立也。为冯太后追福。在开阳门外三里。

[At the Kaiyang Gate] was the Academy for the Sons of the Noblemen of the Han[3], in front of which were the "stone classics" on twenty-five slabs in three different scripts. Engraved on both sides were the two classics, *The Spring and Autumn Annals* and *The Book of Documents*. The three scripts were: seal, kedou and li, which were the calligraphic relics of Cai Yong, the Right Commandant of Palace Squires (You Zhong-lang Jiang) of the Han. Eighteen slabs [of his] still survived, but all the others were either damaged or destroyed.

开阳门御道东有汉国子学堂，堂前有三种字石经二十五碑，表里刻之，写《春秋》《尚书》二部，作篆、科斗、隶三种字，汉右中郎将蔡邕笔之遗迹也。犹有十八碑，馀皆残毁。

In addition, there were forty-eight [other] slabs engraved in li script on both sides, on which were written the four classical works [known respectively as] the *Zhou Yi*, *The Book of Documents*, *The Gong Yang Commentary*, and *The Book of Rites*. Along with an additional monument, "Zan Xue" "In Praise of Studies," they were all erected in front of the hall. Of the six slabs mentioned in

复有石碑四十八枚，亦表里隶书，写《周易》《尚书》《公羊》《礼记》四部。又赞学碑一所，并在堂前。魏文帝作《典论》六碑，至太和十七年犹存四碑。

---

1. Wang Yitong and Cao Hong(trans,), *A Record of Buddhist Monasteries in Luo Yang*, Beijing: Zhong Hua Book Company, 2007, pp. 170–175.
2. The temple was built on the old site of the Ying Shi Cao (Office of Hawks' Trainers), which had been abolished to show the emperor's concern for life.
3. The lecture hall of the academy was built in 51 AD. It was one hundred Chinese feet long and thirty Chinese feet wide. As the title suggests, the Imperial Academy for the Sons of the Noblemen was reserved for members of the nobility, whereas the Imperial Academy (Tai Xue) was open to other candidates.

the Dianlun (*Treatise on Writing*) composed by Emperor
Wen of the Wei, four still survived in 493 AD.

In the fourth year of the Wuding Period (546 AD), [Gao Cheng] had all the "stone classics" moved to Ye[1].	武定四年，大将军迁石经于邺。

Emperor Gao Zu labeled [this area] Quan Xue (Exhortation to Study) Ward. [In] the ward were three temples: the Da Jue (Great Awakening), the San Bao (the Three Precious Ones[2]), and Ning Yuan (To Quell the Distant Regions), surrounded by a orchard that produced such valued fruits as Da Gu (Great Valley[3]) and Cheng Guang (To Accept Light) apricots.	高祖题为劝学里。里内有大觉、三宝、宁远三寺。周回有园，珍果出焉，有大谷梨承光之柰。

The Cheng Guang Temple also produced many other fruits, but the apricots were the most delicious and without equal in the capital.	承光寺亦多果木，柰味甚美，冠于京师。

To the east of the Quan Xue Ward was the Yan Xian Ward (Ward of Invitation to the Worthy), in which was the Zheng Jue Nunnery (Perfect Enlightenment Nunnery). It was established by Wang Su (463 AD–501 AD), President of the Department of State Affairs.	劝学里东有延贤里，里内有正觉寺，尚书令王肃所立也。

[Wang] Su, Styled Gong Yi, a native of Lang Ya, was the son of [Wang] Huan, Governor of Yong Zhou of the Qi.	肃字恭懿，琅琊人也，伪齐雍州刺史奂之子也。

Learned and versatile, [Wang] Su was a man with superb skill at letters. In the eighteenth year of the Tai	赠学多通，才辞美茂，为齐秘书丞，太和

---

1. The text attaches this sentence of twelve characters to the next paragraph, but Ji Zheng suggests that it be moved here; hence the translation. The text also gives Ying 颖, which is an obvious error for Ye 邺. The move took place in the eighth month of 546 AD. Fifty-two monuments were involved.
2. That is, Buddha, the Law, and Monastic Discipline.
3. They were also known as "han xiao" (含消, holding in mouth and melt away) pears. It is said that each weighed ten catties (roughly equivalent to 2.22 kilograms), although if such a pear dropped to the ground, it changed into juice.

He period (494 AD), while serving the Ji as Assistant Archivist (Mi Shu Cheng), he deserted the illegitimate and surrendered to the legitimate. At the time, Emperor Gao Zu was building a new capital in Luo Yang, where many reforms were carried out. [Wang] Su, vastly knowledgeable of past events, was tremendously helpful. Emperor Gao Zu held him in high esteem and always called him Master Wang. The name of Yan Xian was adopted because of [Wang] Su.

十八年背逆归顺。时高祖新营洛邑，多所制造，肃博识旧事，大有裨益，高祖甚重之，常呼王生。延贤之名，因肃立之。

When [Wang] Su was in the south of the Yangtze, he was married to a daughter of a Xie family[1].

After his arrival in the [Wei] capital, he was married again to a princess. Later, Lady Xie became a nun. She too came to join [Wang] Su. [Knowing that Wang Su had a wife who was a princess[2], his first wife Xie] wrote a five-character poem for [Wang] Su as a gift, which reads:

肃在江南之日，聘谢氏女为妻，

及至京师，复尚公主。谢作五言诗以赠之，其诗曰：

> Hitherto a silkworm on a bamboo stand,
> Now silk in the loom.
> Attached to the spinning wheel and following the spindle,
> Don't you recall the days of intimate relationship [between the silk and worm]?

本为箔上蚕，
今作机上丝。
得路逐胜去，

颇忆缠绵时。

The Princess wrote a poem in reply for [Wang] Su, saying:

公主代肃答谢云：

> The needle lets the thread pass through.
> In its eye it always takes in the silk.
> Now sewing a new piece of fabric,
> How can it accept [the thread] of the past?

针是贯线物，
目中恒任丝。
得帛缝新去，
何能衲故时。

Greatly embarrassed by this, [Wang] Su built the Zheng Jue Nunnery for her to live a secluded life.

肃甚有愧谢之色，
遂造正觉寺以憩之。

---

1. Daughter of Xie Zhuang (谢庄).
2. Young sister of Emperor Gao Zu, who was first enfeoffed as Princess Peng Cheng but later as Princess of Chen Liu (陈留). She was married to Liu Chengxu (刘承绪), son of Liu Chang (刘昶) (435 AD–497 AD), who, like Wang Su, was a deserter from the south. After Liu Chengxu's death, she was remarried to Wang Su.

Extensive Reading B

Selections from the Dunhuang Version of the *Platform Sutra*[1]

敦煌写本
《六祖坛经》
选篇

One day, suddenly and quite unexpectedly, the Fifth Patriarch asked that all his disciples come to him. When they had gathered together, he said, "I say to you that birth and death are great affairs for the people of the world. You disciples practice selfcultivation all day, but all you seek is [rebirth in] blessed realms. You do not seek to escape from the bitter sea of birth and death. Your self-nature deludes you regarding the gateway to blessings; how can it possibly save you? All of you ponder this; return to your rooms and look within yourselves. Those with understanding and insight will grasp for themselves the prajna-wisdom[2] of their original nature. Each of you, write a poem for me. I will look at your compositions, and if there is one among you who is enlightened regarding the great insight[3], I will grant him the robe and the dharma and make him the Sixth Patriarch. Quickly now, make haste!"

祖一日唤诸门人总来。"吾向汝说，世人生死事大，汝等终日只求福田，不求出离生死苦海，自性若迷，福何可救？汝等各去自看智慧，取自本心般若之性，各作一偈，来呈吾看。若悟大意，付汝衣法，为第六代祖。火急速去，不得迟滞！"

That evening, at the third watch [midnight], without anyone's knowledge, the head monk, Shen Xiu, took up a candle and by its light wrote a poem on the middle of the wall in the south corridor. His poem read:

是夜三更，不使人知，自执灯，书偈于南廊壁间，呈心所见。偈曰：

---

1. Philip J. Ivanhoe. *Readings from the Lu-Wang School of Neo-Confucianism*, Cambridge: Hackett Publishing Company, 2009, pp. 14–16.

2. Prajna is the special, liberating wisdom that sees and appreciates that all things ultimately are "empty." For a helpful discussion of this idea, see in Heinrich Dumoulin, India and China, vol. 1 of *Zen Buddhism: A History*. New York: Macmillan, 1988.

3. The "great insight" is the truth of emptiness, which constitutes enlightenment.

The body is the tree of insight (prajna);
The mind is like a clear mirror.
Always clean and polish it;
Never allow dirt or dust!

身是菩提树，
心如明镜台，
时时勤拂拭，
勿使惹尘埃。

    I, Huineng, also composed a poem and asked someone who was literate to write it down for me on the wall of the west corridor as a manifestation of my original mind[1]. ... Unless one recognizes one's original mind, studying the dharma will result in no benefit. If one recognizes one's original mind and sees one's nature, one will be enlightened regarding the great insight. My poem went:

惠能闻己，遂
言："亦有一偈，望别
驾为书。"……不识本
心，学法无益；若识自
本心，见自本性：

Insight originally has no tree;
The bright mirror has no stand.
Buddha-nature is always pure and clean;
How could there ever be dirt or dust?

菩提本无树，
明镜亦非台，
本来无一物，
何处惹尘埃?

---

1. This term finds one of its earliest uses in Mencius, where it referred to ones innate, nascent moral sensibilities. It was taken up and used extensively by neo-Confucians. Here, it refers to an innate and perfect Buddha-mind or Buddha-nature. It was thought by the translator Philip J. Ivanhoe to contain faculties of cognition and emotion as well as intention or volition. In some contexts, one or another of these various senses may dominate, but often all are present to some degree. The reader is advised to judge by context where the emphasis falls in a given case.

Extensive Reading C

Buddhist Influence on Chinese Religious Life[1]

Hu Shi

Section III

The introduction of Buddhism undoubtedly brought about a tremendous change in the religious life of the Chinese nation. A practical and matter-of-fact race was gradually worked up to religious enthusiasm, even to religious fanaticism. Temples and stupas were built everywhere; men and women deserted their families to become monks and nuns. The monumental stone sculptures at Da Tong and Long Men testify to this day to the height of zeal of the Buddhistic age.

With this sudden outburst of religious enthusiasm, there also came the worst features of Mahayana Buddhism. Extreme forms of asceticism and self-torture were commonly practiced. We may remember that one of the chapters of the *Saddharma Pundarika* contains the idea that the most effective kind of sacrifice is the sacrifice of one's own body. The hero of that chapter therefore perfumed his whole body, anointed it with fragrant oil, soaked all clothing in oil, and finally burned himself as a sacrifice to Buddha. The Saddharma Pundarika was exceedingly popular, and the idea of bodily sacrifice was soon taken up by the fanatical monks. The Confucianist philosopher Hu Yin recorded a number of such cases in his *anti-Buddhistic treatise*. The monk Hui Shao resolved to imitate the Yowang Pu-sa and burned his own body. Another monk, Seng Yu, collected dry faggots into a shrine, seated himself in it, and set fire to it while loudly reciting the Yowang chapter in the *Saddharma Pundarika*. Another monk Bao Ya bound his fingers with oiled cloth and set fire to them. When asked if he felt the pain, he answered "Pain arises from the mind; and when the mind feels no pain, how can the fingers feel pain?" After this trial he piled up dry wood in his storeyed house, coated the walls of his room with oil and, holding a torch with his fingerless arms, set fire to the room.

---

1. This term finds one of its earliest uses in Mencius, where it referred to ones innate, nascent moral sensibilities. It was taken up and used extensively by neo-Confucians. Here, it refers to an innate and perfect Buddha-mind or Buddha-nature. It was thought by the translator Philip J. Ivanhoe to contain faculties of cognition and emotion as well as intention or volition. In some contexts, one or another of these various senses may dominate, but often all are present to some degree. The reader is advised to judge by context where the emphasis falls in a given case.

He was seen performing the ritual of reverent worship amidst the choking smoke. His face and body caught the fire after the second worshipping. Still he continued his ritual, and fell dead upon the burning charcoal!

Section IV

The new religion of Buddhism came to China with irresistible force. Persecution after persecution failed, and Buddhism continued to be the most powerful religion of China. Confucianism was no longer considered as a religion, but as a system of practical ethical and political principles. Buddhism being an ultra-mundane religion, it was necessary to leave the state affairs to the hands of officials trained in the ethico-political philosophy of Confucianism. The only rival religion with which Buddhism often came into conflict was the newly-arisen Daoism. Many of the great persecutions of Buddhism were brought about by the Daoists. Yet the undeniable influence of Buddhism may be seen in every stage of the development of Daoism as a popular religion. Indeed, Daoism may even be described as a religious product of Chinese nationalism—a child which was born in the days of Buddhist triumph and nurtured in the atmosphere of Buddhism, but which grew up with a determination to battle its alien tutor and rival with his own weapons.

Daoism had been a religion of asceticism and magic, but with no organization nor commonly recognized scriptures. Under the influence of the Buddhistic Church organization and Buddhistic Tripitaka, the Daoists began to organize themselves into a church with priests as officials, and to produce a large number of Daoist scriptures. The greatest organizer of Daoism was Kou Qianzhi who, under the patronage of Emperor Xiao Wu of North Wei, established the first Daoist church in Da Tong. The church began with a priesthood of 120 and had its rules regulating the daily and monthly rituals of worship and fasting. This was the first time that ascetic Daoism of the mountains and grottoes suddenly became the established state religion of metropolitan life.

The Daoist scriptures were largely imitations after the Buddhist sutras. The work of imitation began as early as the year 300 AD when a Daoist wrote the *Sutras of Laozi's Conversion of India*. The attempt was to make Buddhism a form of Daoism, and Buddha a convert to Laozi. The fact that Chinese Buddhists persisted in dating the birth of Buddha in the tenth century BC, instead of a later date, was chiefly due to the desire on the part of Chinese Buddhists to make Buddha as old as possible in order to avoid the possibility of his being converted by Laozi into Daoism! As we glance over the several hundred titles in the Daoist Canon now being published by the Commercial Press, we cannot fail to perceive the shameless work of imitation and forgery that has produced this vast amount of parrot-like nonsense! Even the form and style of the Buddhist sutras are retained in many of these Daoist texts. I quote the following opening passage from *The Sutra of Sixteen Books*:

> At that time the Supreme Jade Emperor was in the Lin Xiao Palace of
> the Dou Su Heaven (that is, the Tushita Heaven of Buddhism). Together
> with the Sacred Mother of Yao Chi, he was preaching the Precious Truth
> (Saddharma) of the Great Beginning, the Grand Mean, and the Universal
> Salvation. Among those present were the Five Grand Old Emperors, and
> the Immortals of the Ten Continents, the Three Islands, the Five Sacred
> Mountains, the Four Lakes, and the Three Worlds. All were listening
> to the Precious Truth. At that time, the Emperor of the Eastern Sacred
> Mountain arose from the rank and said: ...

Study Questions

1. How does *The Disposition of Error* argue for the canonization of Buddhism? Do you agree with the arguments? If you have any additions, how would you make them?

2. Compare *An Explanation of the Diagram of the Great Ultimate with the Confirmation of the Consciousness-Only System*, and tell how they each explain the happening and characteristics of nature and humanity.

3. Samsara and Nirvana are two of the most important concepts in Dharma, the law of the universe as taught by Buddha. Samsara refers to the relentless cycle of beings of forms of life with unhappiness and war with themselves, and Nirvana means the end of the cycles, an imperturbable stillness. Can you find similar representations of these two ideas from *The Disposition of Error*? Are there slight differences between the original concepts and the renditions in this essay? What do you think have caused such differences?

4. What historical contexts does Chapter 3 of *A Record of Buddhist Monasteries in Luo Yang* present with regard to the development of Chinese Buddhism during the Southern and Northern Dynasties (420 to 589)? Is there any clue to find the relationship between Buddhism and Confucianism in the text?

5. Do a research on the historical development of Chinese Buddhism, regarding its origin, translation, and indigenous sects and their ideas.

CHAPTER ⑤

The "Others" in Chinese Classics

1. Legalism, as we know, gained authority after it had worked as the tool to help the establishment of Qin sovereignty around 221 BC. Yet when *Si Ku Quan Shu* (*Complete Library of the Four Treasuries*) was compiled late in the eighteenth century, of the 3457 works included, only eight were by the Legalist. How to understand the diminishing influence of legalism in Chinese culture?

2. The "Way" (Dao) seems to be the ultimate pursuit for almost all Chinese schools of thought, despite its varied meanings in different lights. Go back to the main propositions of Confucianism, Daoism, and Chinese Buddhism, and figure out how they interpret the "Way" in different ways. And then, through reading the other schools' ideas as excerpted in this chapter, find their implications of the "Way" from their standpoints.

Introduction

The three dominating schools of thought that are believed to have shaped Chinese classical culture, Confucianism, Daoism, and Chinese Buddhism, could not have been regarded as the dominant without them being counterbalanced and contested by the "others" of Chinese culture. The "others," mostly the Mohism, Legalism, and the Nominalist and Dialectician schools that have come down through history to us, provide Chinese culture with the feature of diversity, together with possibilities to gain more intimacy with its Western counterpart.

Chinese humanity would have been less distinguishable without Confucianism defining its ethical values against the Mohist "Ren" (humanly love) and "Yi" (righteousness). Different from Confucian gradation of love, or what we have termed as "compassion extension," the Mohist "universal love" for the sake of everybody's profit and its antagonism toward wars were based upon a religious utilitarianism, believing that whatever deprived human beings of happiness, life, and material good was offensive to the Supreme Spirit. The humanly love should not be limited within or extended from among families, but should be naturally offered to all human beings, transcending social classes and blood lines. Thus the Mohist "Ren" was colored with a supernatural and egalitarian aura, asking for a more rigid organization of its followers in which they practiced asceticism and communalism.

Sounding quite akin to various western religions, Mohism was obviously counter-intuitive to the Chinese mind in its early history. While Confucius looked to Zhou Dynasty as the model of ideal social organization, Mozi took Xia Dynasty as his model, yet the primitive worship of the supernatural being just ran counter to the spirit of the Spring and Autumn and Warring States Periods, an age that was so intellectually dynamic that yielded "one hundred schools of thought." And the Mohist emphasis of the authority of its own organizational leaders and its abandoning of personal feelings that were believed to stand in the way of positive productivity not only made itself less appealing to the aristocratic but also provoked critiques from other schools of philosophers, with Zhuangzi being one of them commenting that Mohism was "contrary to the hearts of all men."

Similar with Mohism, the loss of popularity with the Legalist school and the Nominalist and Dialectitian schools serves as a foil for explaining the thriving of the more popular ones and thus the features of Chinese culture. The Nominalist and Dialectitian schools, whose debating over metaphysical issues as existence, relativity, space, time, quality, actuality, and causes have not been well preserved to today, suffered a doom out of a similar reason with Mohism. While Mohism was indulged in an ideal that was too far away from its contemporaries, the Logicians were too engaged with concepts that were not well concerned by the Chinese, thus inviting, similarly again with Mohism, such a comment from Zhuangzi, "They are able to subdue other people's mouths, but cannot win their hearts. This is where their narrowness lies." If we conclude that the Mohists and Logicans were both too extreme in their ideas to be practically fitted into a Chinese mind that intended on pragmatism, then how are we to explain the diminishing of Legalism which was once such an important and pragmatic tool to help the first Empire to govern? While reasons may be manifold, its formidable demand for uniformity of thoughts and absolute power of mind-control as seen in its suggestion on the burning of books were rather predicative of its failure in later Chinese intellectual history.

It is undeniable that the "others" in Chinese ancient schools of thought did lack the profound philosophy and broad mindedness of Confucianism, Daoism and Chinese Buddhism, yet they have all contributed to the richness of Chinese culture. Most preciously, they suggest a somewhat subsumed tendency of Chinese epistemology, the pursuit of knowledge for knowledge's own sake. We see from the excerpts of this chapter that Mohism, Legalism and the Logicians were more sincere and committed in pure logical thinking, though all aiming at offering a solid foundation for their own doctrines. For instance, to rectify names carried ethical purposes to Confucius, yet to bring names and actuality into accordance was a more analytic and logical issue in itself either to Han Feizi or Gong Sun Long. The genuine intellectual activity echoed with the golden age philosophy in Western civilization, and thus bridged Chinese culture with the world's, which partly explains why in Modern China, these "others" in ancient classics have become even more attractive worldwide.

Selected Passages from *The Mohist Canons*[1]

《墨经》选篇

Analogism: If A is B and B is C, then it is an inevitable result that A is C; but if A is B but B is not C, then it is not an inevitable insult that A is C. An inevitable result comes from a matching analogy.

The set of "four-legged animal" is larger than "ox" or "horse" and smaller than "animal." Everything belongs to different sets, which can be larger or smaller.

Both the mare and the deer belong to the same large category (the four legged animal). When the mare and the deer are fighting, there may be more than two four-legged animals in the fight. There is difference between "two animals are fighting" and "two small categories of four-legged animals are fighting." The embryo, the liver and the lung are all parts of a mother's body, yet "the love for one's child" is different from "the love of one's body." Both the orange and the cogon may serve as food, yet the former is food for man and the latter is sacrifice to god. The white horse is almost white; you can "examine a horse" but you cannot "almost examine" it. Beauty may not expose itself, so "the beautiful" may not always be "the extravagant."

A man with weak points may not be weak; a man in husbandry may not be a husband; the straw to make sandals is not a sandal. When a whole is divided into two parts, it exists no longer as a whole but as the two parts generated thereof.

If the name and the substance coincide, the object is called rightfully by that name; if the name and the substance do not coincide, the object cannot be rightfully called by that name. Let's take "flower" and "beautiful" as an example. Something that is called a flower is beautiful; something else that is called by some other name is not

止，彼以此其然也，说是其然也；我以此其不然也，疑是其然也。此然是必然，则俱。

谓：四足兽，与生鸟与，物尽与，大小也。

为麋同名，俱斗，不俱二，二与斗也。

包、肝、肺、子，爱也。
橘茅，食与招也。
白马多白，视马不多视，白与视也。
为丽不必丽，不必丽与暴也。

为非以是不为非，若为夫勇不为夫，为屦以买不为屦，夫与屦也。二与一亡，不与一在，偏去之。

有文实也，而后谓之；无文实也，则无谓也。若敷与美，谓是，则是固美也，谓他，则是非美，无谓则疑也。

1. Wang Rongpei and Wang Hong, *The Mohist Canons*, Shanghai: Shanghai Foreign Language Education Publishing House, 2010.

beautiful. Without proper names, there comes uncertainty.

In terms of the features of an object, what can be seen and what cannot be seen are not separable from each other. For example, width and length coexist in the same plane; hardness and whiteness coexist in the same stone.

见不见不离，一二相盈，广修，坚白。

He who can lift a weight but does not pick up a needle is not to be blamed, if it is not the duty of a strong man. Guessing at whether a handful of items is in the odd number or in the even number is not the duty of a mathematician. The ears can hear but cannot see while the eyes can see but cannot hear.

举不重，不与箴，非力之任也。为握者之觭倍，非智之任也。若耳目异。

Which is longer, a plank of wood or a night? Which do you possess more, wisdom or grains? Which is more valuable, rank or parents or virtue or price? Which is taller, the height of a deer or the flight of a crane? Which is more sorrowful, the chirrup of a cicada or the music of a zither?

木与夜孰长，智与粟孰多，爵、亲、行、贾，四者孰贵？麋与霍孰高？蚓与瑟孰瑟？

The total volume of the removed part plus the remaining part is the same as the whole.

偏，俱一无变。

Loan-name: A loan-name is certainly a name loaned to name something else; otherwise, it would not have been called a loanname. A dog with the loan-name of "crane" is not a crane.

假必非也而后假。狗假霍也，犹氏霍也。

...

......

It is admissible to call something by the loan-name of "crane." As something with the loan-name of "crane" is not a crane, to say that something with the loan-name of "crane" is a crane is not admissible. The name I give to an object must agree with the name another person gives to the object. If the loan-name I use in naming an object agrees with what he uses, my loan-name will do. If what I use to name an object does not agree with what he uses to name the object, what I use to name the object will not do.

惟，谓是霍可，而犹之非夫霍也，谓彼是是也。不可谓者，毋惟乎其谓。彼犹惟乎其谓，则吾谓不行。彼若不惟其谓，则不行也。

If the south has a limit, the number of people is exhaustible; if the south does not have a limit, the number of people is inexhaustible. If whether or not the south has a limit is unknown, we will not know whether the number of people is exhaustible or not. If we do not know whether the people have filled the universe or not, we do

无，南者有穷则可尽，无穷则不可尽。有穷无穷未可智，则可尽不可尽未可智。人之盈之否未可智，而人之可尽不可尽亦未可智。

not know whether the number of people is exhaustible or not. Then, is it mistaken to hold the view that we can love all the people in the universe? If the people cannot fill the limitless universe, the number of people will be exhaustible. Therefore, we can love an exhaustible number of people and the view of universal love is not mistaken. If the people can fill the limitless universe, the number of people will be inexhaustible. Therefore, we can love an inexhaustible number of people and the view of universal love is not mistaken.

How can we love the people all over the universe without knowing their number? What if we miss some of the people in our count? If we count all people we know, we love all the people we know. This is universal love. Therefore, there is no doubt about the view that we can love all the people although we do not know their number.

Benevolence: To be benevolent is to love others and to be righteous is to benefit others. I bestow love and benefit upon others while others receive my love and benefit. As both the love and benefit I bestow upon others are from within, we cannot say that the love is from within and the benefit is from without. As both the love and the benefit others receive are from without, we cannot say the love is from within and the benefit is from without. In view of "benevolence from within and righteousness from without," love is cited as an example of being within and benefit is cited as an example of being without. These examples are partial. In the same way, the statement "you exhale with your left nostril and inhale with your right nostril" is a self-contradiction.

Learning: Thinking that people do not know "It is useless to learn," those who are against learning tell them about this. But to make people know about this is actually to teach them to learn about this. Those are in the wrong that take learning as useless on the one hand and teach people to learn on the other.

Criticism: Here is a comment on whether something is to be criticized or not. If something ought to be criticized as a result of logical reasoning, the criticism

而必人之可尽爱也，悖。人若不盈无穷，则人有穷也。尽有穷无难。盈无穷，则无穷尽也，尽无穷无难。

不，不智其数，恶智爱民之尽之也？或者遗乎其问也？尽问人则尽爱其所问，若不智其数而智爱之尽之也，无难。

仁，仁爱也。义，利也。爱利，此也。所爱所利，彼也。爱利不相为内外，所爱利亦不相为外内。其为仁内也，义外也，举爱与所利也，是狂举也。若左目出右目入。

学，以为不知学之无益也，故告之也，是。使智学之无益也，是教也，以学为无益也教，悖。

论诽，诽之可不可，以理之可诽，虽多诽，其诽是也；其理不

is correct no matter how much criticism is given; if something ought not to be criticized as a result of logical reasoning, the criticism is correct no matter how little criticism is given. When someone says that there should not be too much criticism, he seems to be comparing something long with something short.

可非，虽少诽，今也谓多诽者不可，是犹以长论短。

If you attack other people's criticism, you are making criticism yourself and your own criticism should be attacked too. If you accept other people's criticism, your mistake can be exposed to criticism. Being open to criticism helps you to consolidate your arguments.

非诽，非己之诽也。不非诽，非可非也。不可非也，是不非诽也。

Selected Passages from *Han Feizi*[1]

There are four things that enable the enlightened ruler to achieve accomplishments and establish fame; namely, timeliness of the seasons, the hearts of the people, skill and talents, and position of power. Without the timeliness of the seasons, even the Yaos cannot grow a single ear of grain in the winter. Acting against the sentiment of the people, even Meng Pen and Xia Yu (famous men of great strength) could not make them exhaust their efforts. Therefore with timeliness of the seasons, the grains will grow of themselves. If the ruler has won the hearts of the people, they will exhort themselves without being pressed. If skill and talents are utilized, results will be quickly achieved without any haste. If one occupies a position of power, his fame will be achieved without pushing forward. Like water flowing and like a boat floating, the ruler follows the course of Nature and enforces an infinite number of commands. Therefore he is called an enlightened ruler.

...

The questioner asks, "Of the doctrines of the two schools of Shen Buhai and Shang Yang, which is of more urgent need to the state?"

I reply: "They cannot be evaluated. A man will die if he does not eat for ten days. He will also die if he wears no clothing during the height of a severe cold spell. If it is asked whether clothing or food is more urgently needed by a man, the reply is that he cannot live without either, for they are both means to preserve life.

Shen Buhai advocated statecraft and Shang Yang advocated law. Statecraft involves appointing officials according to their abilities and demanding that actualities correspond to names. It holds the power of life and death

《韩非子》
选篇

　　明君之所以立功成名者四：一曰天时，二曰人心，三曰技能，四曰势位。非天时，虽十尧不能冬生一穗；逆人心，虽贲、育不能尽人力。故得天时则不务而自生，得人心，则不趣而自劝；因技能则不急而自疾；得势位则不推进而名成。若水之流，若船之浮。守自然之道，行毋穷之令，故曰明主。

　　……

　　问者曰："申不害、公孙鞅，此二家之言孰急于国？"

　　应之曰："是不可程也。人不食，十日则死；大寒之隆，不衣亦死。谓之衣食孰急于人，则是不可一无也，皆养生之具也。

　　今申不害言术而公孙鞅为法。术者，因任而授官，循名而责实，操杀生之柄，课群臣之能者也。此人主之所执

1. Wing-Tsit Chan, *A Source Book in Chinese Philosophy*, Princeton: Princeton University Press, 1969, p. 255.

and inquires into the ability of all ministers. These are powers held by the ruler. By law is meant statutes and orders formulated by the government, with punishments which will surely impress the hearts of the people. Rewards are there for those who obey the law and punishments are to be imposed on those who violate orders. These are things the ministers must follow. On the higher level, if the ruler has no statecraft, he will be mined. On the lower level, if ministers are without laws, they will become rebellious. Neither of these can be dispensed with. They both are means of emperors and kings. ..."

The means by which the enlightened ruler controls his ministers are none other than the two handles. The two handles are punishment and kindness.

What do we mean by punishment and kindness? To execute is called punishment and to offer congratulations or rewards is called kindness. Ministers are afraid of execution and punishment but look upon congratulations and rewards as advantages. Therefore, if a ruler himself applies punishment and kindness, all ministers will fear his power and turn to the advantages. As to treacherous ministers, they are different. They would get [the handle of punishment] from the ruler [through flattery and so forth] and punish those whom they hate and get [the handle of kindness] from the ruler and reward those, whom they love. If the ruler does not see to it that the power of reward and punishment proceeds from himself but instead leaves it to his ministers to apply reward and punishment, then everyone in the state will fear the ministers and slight the ruler, turn to them and get away from the ruler. This is the trouble of the ruler who loses the handles of punishment and kindness.

For the tiger is able to subdue the dog because of its claws and fangs. If the tiger abandons its claws and fangs and lets the dog use them, it will be subdued by the dog. Similarly, the ruler controls his ministers through punishment and kindness. If the ruler abandons his punishment and kindness and lets his ministers use them,

也。法者，宪令著于官府，刑罚必于民心，赏存乎慎法，而罚加乎奸令者也。此臣之所师也。君无术则弊于上，臣无法则乱于下，此不可一无，皆帝主之具也。"……

明主之所道制其臣者，二柄而已矣。二柄者，刑德也。

何谓刑德？曰：杀戮之谓刑，庆赏之谓德。为人臣者畏诛罚而利庆赏，故人主自用其刑德，则群臣畏其威而归其利矣。故世之奸臣则不然，所恶，则能得之其主而罪之；所爱，则能得之其主而赏之；今人主非使赏罚之威利出于己也，听其臣而行其赏罚，则一国之人皆畏其臣而易其君，归其臣而去其君矣。此人主失刑德之患也。

夫虎之所以能服狗者，爪牙也。使虎释其爪牙而使狗用之，则虎反服于狗矣。人主者，以刑德制臣者也。今君人者释其刑德而使臣

he will be controlled by the ministers....[1]

When a ruler wants to suppress treachery, he must examine the correspondence between actuality and names. Actuality and names refer to the ministers' words and deeds. When a minister presents his words, the ruler assigns him a task in accordance with his words and demands accomplishments specifically from that work. If the results correspond to the task and the task to the words, he should be rewarded. If the accomplishments do not correspond to the task or the task not to the words, he will be punished. If the minister's words are big but his accomplishment is small, he will be punished. The punishment is not for the small accomplishment but for the fact that the accomplishment does not correspond to the words. If the minister's words are small and his accomplishments are big, he will also be punished. It is not that the ruler is not pleased with the big accomplishments but he considers the failure of the big accomplishments to correspond to the words worse than the big accomplishments themselves. Therefore he is to be punished[2].

用之，则君反制于臣矣。……

人主将欲禁奸，则审合刑名者，言异事也。为人臣者陈而言，君以其言授之事，专以其事责其功。功当其事，事当其言，则赏；功不当其事，事不当其言，则罚。故群臣其言大而功小者则罚，非罚小功也，罚功不当名也；群臣其言小而功大者亦罚，非不说于大功也，以为不当名也害甚于有大功，故罚。

---

1. Comment from the translator: Confucius was not unaware of the "two handles" of the government. But whereas the Confucians put virtue ahead of punishment, the Legalists put punishment ahead of virtue. In fact, virtue in the true sense of the word is rejected by the Legalists, for de as used here by Han Feizi no longer denotes moral virtue but merely kindness in the sense of rewards and favors. Even these are to be bestowed with an ulterior motive.

2. Comment from the translator: Like practically all ancient Chinese schools, the Legalists emphasized the theory of the correspondence of names and actualities. But while the Confucians stressed the ethical and social meaning of the theory and the Logicians stressed the logical aspect, the Legalists were interested in it primarily for the purpose of political control. With them the theory is neither ethical nor logical but a technique for regimentation.

"Memorial on the Burning of Books" from "Li Si" of the *Records of the Historian*[1]

《史记·李斯列传》
选篇

In earlier times the empire disintegrated and fell into disorder, and no one was capable of unifying it. Thereupon the various feudal lords rose to power. In their discourses they all praised the past in order to disparage the present and embellished empty words to confuse the truth. Everyone cherished his own favorite school of learning and criticized what has been instituted by the authorities. But at present Your Majesty possesses a unified empire, has regulated the distinction of black and white, and has firmly established for yourself a position of sole supremacy. And yet these independent schools, joining with each other, criticize the codes of laws and instructions. Hearing of the promulgation of a decree, they criticize it, each from the standpoint of his own school. At home they disapprove of it in their hearts; going out they criticize it in the thoroughfare. They seek a reputation by discrediting their sovereign; they appear superior by expressing contrary views, and they lead the lowly multitude in the spading of slander. If such license is not prohibited, the sovereign power will decline above and partisan factions will form below. It would be well to prohibit this.

古者天下散乱，莫能相一，是以诸侯并作，语皆道古以害今，饰虚言以乱实，人善其所私学，以非上所建立。今陛下并有天下，别白黑而定一尊；而私学乃相与非法教之制，闻令下，即各以其私学议之，入则心非，出则巷议，非主以为名，异趣以为高，率群下以造谤。如此不禁，则主势降乎上，党与成乎下。禁之便。

Your servant suggests that all books in the imperial archives, save the memoirs of Qin, be burned. All persons in the empire, except members of the Academy or Learned Scholars, in possession of *The Book of Odes*, *The Book of History*, and discourses of the hundred philosophers should take them to the local governors and have them indiscriminately burned. Those who dare to talk to each other about *The Book of Odes* and *The Book of History* should be executed and their bodies exposed in the market

臣请诸有文学诗书百家语者，蠲除去之。令到满三十日弗去，黥为城旦。所不去者，医药卜筮种树之书。若有欲学者，以吏为师。

---

1. Wm. Theodore de Bary, Wing-Tsit Chan, and Burton Watson, *Sources of Chinese Tradition*, New York: Columbia University Press, 1960, pp. 140–141.

place. Anyone referring to the past to criticize the present should, together with all members of his family, be put to death. Officials who fail to report cases that have come under their attention are equally guilty. After thirty days from the time of issuing the decree, those who have not destroyed their books are to be branded and sent to build the Great Wall. Books not to be destroyed will be those on medicine and pharmacy, divination by the tortoise and milfoil, and agriculture and arboriculture. People wishing to pursue learning should take the officials as their teachers.

A Selection from *Gongsun Longzi* on the "White Horse"[1]

《公孙龙子·白马论》选篇

A: Is it correct to say that a white horse is not a horse?

B: It is.

A: Why?

B: Because "horse" denotes the form and "white" denotes the color. What denotes the color does not denote the form. Therefore we say that a white horse is not a horse.

A: There being a horse, one cannot say that there is no horse. If one cannot say that there is no horse, then isn't [it] a horse? Since there being a white horse means that there is a horse, why does being white make it not a horse?

B: Ask for a horse, and neither a yellow nor a black one may answer. Ask for a white horse, and neither the yellow horse nor the black one may answer. If a white horse were a horse, then what is asked in both cases would be the same. If what is asked is the same, then a white horse would be no different from a horse. If what is asked is no different, then why is it that yellow and black horses may yet answer in the one case but not in the other? Clearly the two cases are incompatible. Now the yellow horse and the black horse remain the same. And yet they answer to a horse but not to a white horse. Obviously a white horse is not a horse.

A: You consider a horse with color as not a horse. Since there is no horse in the world without color, is it all right [to say] that there is no horse in the world?

B: Horses of course have color. Therefore there are white horses. If horses had no color, there would be simply horses. Where do white horses come in? Therefore whiteness is different from horse. A white horse means a

曰：白马非马，可乎？

曰：可。

曰：何哉？

曰：马者，所以命形也；白者，所以命色也。命色者非名形也。故曰："白马非马"。

曰：有马不可谓无马也。不可谓无马者，非马也？有白马为有马，白之，非马何也？

曰：求马，黄、黑马皆可致；求白马，黄、黑马不可致。是白马乃马也，是所求一也。所求一者，白者不异马也，所求不异，如黄、黑马有可有不可，何也？可与不可，其相非明。如黄、黑马一也，而可以应有马，而不可以应有白马，是白马之非马，审矣！

曰：以马之有色为非马，天下非有无色之马。天下无马可乎？

曰：马固有色，故有白马。使马无色，有马如已耳，安取白马？故白马非马也。白马

1. Wing-Tsit Chan, *A Source Book in Chinese Philosophy*, Princeton: Princeton University Press, 1969, pp. 235–237.

horse combined with whiteness. [Thus in one case it is] horse and [in the other it is] a white horse. Therefore we say that a white horse is not a horse.

A: [Since you say that] before the horse is combined with whiteness, it is simply a horse, before whiteness is combined with a horse it is simply whiteness, and when the horse and whiteness are combined they are collectively called a white horse, you are calling a combination by what is not a combination. This is incorrect. Therefore it is incorrect to say that a white horse is not a horse.

B: If you regard a white horse as a horse, is it correct to say that a white horse is a yellow horse?

A: No.

B: If you regard a white horse as different from a yellow horse, you are differentiating a yellow horse from a horse. To differentiate a yellow horse from a horse is to regard the yellow horse as not a horse. Now to regard a yellow horse as not a horse and yet to regard a white horse as a horse is like a bird flying into a pool or like the inner and outer coffins being in different places. This would be the most contradictory argument and the wildest talk.

A: [When we say that] a white horse cannot be said to be not a horse, we are separating the whiteness from the horse. If [the whiteness] is not separated from [the horse], then there would be a white horse and we should not say that there is [just] a horse. Therefore when we say that there is a horse, we do so singly because it is a horse and not because it is a white horse. When we say that there is a horse, we do not mean that there are a horse [as such] and another horse [as the white horse].

B: It is all right to ignore the whiteness that is not fixed on any object. But in speaking of the white horse, we are talking about the whiteness that is fixed on the object. The object on which whiteness is fixed is not whiteness [itself]. The term "horse" does not involve any choice of color and therefore either a yellow horse or a black one may answer. But the term "white horse" does involve a choice of color. Both the yellow horse and the black one are excluded because of their color. Only a white horse

者，马与白也。黑与白，马也？故曰白马非马也。

曰：马未与白为马，白未与马为白。合马与白，复名白马。是相与以不相与为名，未可。故曰：白马非马未可。

曰：以"有白马为有马"，谓有白马为有黄马，可乎？

曰：未可。

曰：以有马为异有黄马，是异黄马与马也；异黄马与马，是以黄为非马。以黄马为非马，而以白马为有马，此飞者入池而棺椁异处，此天下之悖言辞也。

曰：以有白马不可谓无马者，离白之谓也；不离者有白马不可谓有马也。故所以为有马者，独以马为有马耳，非以白马为有马耳。故其为有马也，不可以谓"白马"也。

曰：以白者不定所白，忘之而可也。白马者，言白定所白也，定所白者非白也。马者，无去取于色，故黄、黑皆所以应；白马者，有去取于色，黄、黑马皆所以色去，故唯白马独可以应耳。无去者非有

may answer. What does not exclude [color] is not the same as what excludes [color]. Therefore we say that a white horse is not a horse.

去也，故曰："白马非马"。

Implications of Chinese Epistemology[1]

Frederick W. Mote

Were we to review all the other known philosophies of the Golden Age, we would find in most of them practical concern for the problem of order in society, efforts to establish theories of human nature, and philosophic justifications for particular patterns of living. We would find but little speculation just for speculation's sake. China had a distinct dearth of "pure philosophers" who spun out theories about abstract philosophical issues. But as the foregoing discussions of Mohism and the logicians show, some ancient Chinese thinkers did consider the formal problems of logic and had the ability to deal with epistemological issues in a fairly advanced and sophisticated manner. The lack of further development in China, therefore, reflects a choice.

Yet Chinese thought had its characteristic mode, one that was quite different from the modes of classical Greek, ancient Indian, and other notable early philosophic traditions. What caused China's distinctiveness? Is the "cosmological gulf" between China and the rest of the world, if it can be considered fully established, sufficient explanation of all these further points of distinctiveness? Or is the cosmological gulf itself merely part of a cultural set, the whole of which demands more fundamental explanation of its distinctiveness, or of its Chineseness?

Coupled with the characteristic mode of Chinese thought, as illustrated in its handling of the problem of knowledge, are several other distinctive features of Chinese intellectual history. Many scholars have noted these, and some have attempted to formulate explanations based on comparisons with Western intellectual history. Joseph Needham has observed certain cases in the history of Chinese mathematical and astronomical sciences where the ancient Chinese adopted solutions conceptually quite different from, but not necessarily scientifically inferior to, those adopted in the West. Chinese mathematics was from its beginnings more algebraic, whereas Greek mathematics was more geometric in character. Again, Chinese astronomy was polar and equatorial in conception and method, whereas Western astronomy was ecliptic. Wolfram Eberhard quotes

---

1.   Frederick W. Mote, *Intellectual Foundations of China*, New York: Alfred A. Knopf, 1971, pp. 106–109.

Needham: "If, like all Chinese science, Chinese astronomy was fundamentally empirical and observational, it was spared the excesses and aberrations, as well as the triumphs, of Occidental theorizing."[1]

We may also observe that the development of epistemological and metaphysical theory in classical Greek thought came after a prior interest in and development of mathematics. Pythagoras antedated Socrates by a century and a half. In China, the great interest in and development of mathematics occurred in the Han dynasty, some centuries after the Golden philosophy had more or less fixed the characteristic mode in thought. So the sequence of these developments was reversed. But does this observation explain anything?

The Polish historian of Chinese thought, Januz Chmielewski, notes a preoccupation with the concept and significance of nonidentity in early Chinese logic: this contrasts in his mind with Greek logicians' functionally analogous but qualitatively different focus on the concept of identity, as in the syllogism.

Throughout this book we have stressed the perceptiveness of psychological observation and the unifying preoccupation with the psychological element in almost all early Chinese schools of thought. All these generalized observations display the distinctiveness of Chinese thought. What, however, do they contribute to explaining that distinctiveness? Moreover, do they bear in any way on the generally noted Chinese preference for the practical, the applied aspects as opposed to the more theoretical approach of Western philosophy?

While it by no means offers a comprehensive or wholly satisfactory explanation of what makes Chinese thought distinctive, the fact that all schools of Chinese thought have looked with great suspicion upon the concern with any purely speculative theory of knowledge disputatiously maintained (was the association of theory and dispute necessary?) must have acted as a major deterrent to the development of such fields of inquiry, and that constriction must be judged to have affected the profile of Chine thought markedly. At the same time this unwillingness to argue about theory displays further the characteristic mind-set of the early Chinese intellectual world; it is in the pattern. We have noted that Confucius's doctrine of the rectification of names had only ethical, not theoretical or epistemological intent.

Similarly, among later thinkers, any concern which did not prove useful in immediate application tended to be rejected. Zhuangzi said: "If we look at Hui Shi's ability from the standpoint of Heaven and Earth, it was only like the restless activity of a mosquito or gadfly; of what service was it to anything?" Xun Zi, who went further than any other Confucian in sharpening the tools

---

1. Quoted in Wolfram Eberhard's review of Needham's work, *Journal of Asian Studies*, 19 (1959), p. 65.

of thinking, nonetheless noted that Hui Shi's teachings "could not serve as the basis for government" and that he "worked much but accomplished little." He concluded that Hui Shi was "blinded by phrases and didn't know realities." The historian Sima Tan, of the second century B.C., although somewhat sympathetic toward Daoism and therefore not so relentlessly practical-minded as the typical orthodox Confucians, complained that Hui Shi "lost sight of human feelings." In the second century A.D., the great Confucian scholar and historian, Ban Gu, though acknowledging that "correct names" are important and that in fact the search for them had been started by Confucius, nevertheless added that, when the search becomes disputatious, it creates only division and disorder. With him, as characteristically with all later Confucians, order and practical social good were more important in any philosophy than a search for abstract truth.

So one implication we can clearly derive as we review the problem of knowledge is that the cultural values of the civilization are thoroughly intertwined with the development of its intellectual history. Another is that we can describe much more than we can explain at this stage in our knowledge of early China. The characteristic mode is clear; it causes, much less so.

Extensive Reading B

Selections from *The Spirit of the Chinese People*[1]

Gu Hongming

In the first early and rude stage of society, mankind had to use physical force to subdue and subjugate human passions. Thus hordes of savages had to be subjugated by sheer physical force. But as civilization advances, mankind discovers a force more potent and more effective for subduing and controlling human passions than physical force and this force is called moral force. The moral force which in the past has been effective in subduing and controlling the human passions in the population of Europe, is Christianity. But now this war[2] with the armament preceding it, seems to show that Christianity has become ineffective as a moral force. Without an effective moral force to control and restrain human passions, the people of Europe have had again to employ physical force to keep civil order. As Carlyle truly says, "Europe is Anarchy plus a constable." The use of physical force to maintain civil order leads to militarism. In fact militarism is necessary in Europe today because of the want of an effective moral force. But militarism leads to war and war means destruction and waste. Thus the people of Europe are on the horns of a dilemma. If they do away with militarism, anarchy will destroy their civilization, but if they keep up militarism, their civilization will collapse through the waste and destruction of war. But Englishmen say that they are determined to put down Prussian militarism and Lord Kitchner believes that he will be able to stamp out Prussian militarism with three million drilled and armed Englishmen. But then it seems to me when Prussian militarism is thus stamped out, there will then arise another militarism, —the British militarism which again will have to be stamped out. Thus there seems to be no way of escape out of this vicious circle.

But is there really no way of escape? Yes, I believe there is. The American Emerson long ago said, "I can easily see the bankruptcy of the vulgar musket worship, —though great men be musket worshipers; and 'tis certain, as God liveth, the gun that does need another gun, the law of love and justice alone can effect a clean revolution'." Now if the people of Europe really want to put down militarism,

---

1. Gu Hongming, *The Spirit of the Chinese People*, Beijing: City Press, 2008.
2. WWI.

there is only one way of doing it and that is, to use what Emerson calls the gun that does not need another gun, the law of love and justice, —in fact, moral force. With an effective moral force, militarism will become unnecessary and disappear of itself. But now, that Christianity has become ineffective as a moral force the problem is where are the people of Europe to find this new effective moral force which will make militarism unnecessary?

I believe the people of Europe will find this new moral force in China, —in the Chinese civilization. The moral force in the Chinese civilization which can make militarism unnecessary is the Religion of good citizenship. But people will say to me, "There have also been wars in China." It is true there have been wars in China; but, since the time of Confucius 2500 years ago, we Chinese have had no militarism such as that we see in Europe today. In China war is an accident, whereas in Europe war has become a necessity. We Chinese are liable to have wars, but we do not live in constant expectation of war. In fact the one thing intolerable in the state of Europe, it seems to me, is not so much war as the fact that everybody is constantly afraid that his neighbor as soon as he gets strong enough to be able to do it, will come to rob and murder him and he has therefore to arm himself or pay for an armed policeman to protect him. Thus what weighs upon the people of Europe is not so much the accident of War, but the constant necessity to arm themselves, the absolute necessity to use physical force to protect themselves.

Now in China because we Chinese have the Religion of good citizenship a man does not feel the need of using physical force to protect himself; he has seldom the need even to call in and use the physical force of the policeman, of the State to protect him. A man in China is protected by the sense of justice of his neighbor; he is protected by the readiness of his fellow men to obey the sense of moral obligation. In fact, a man in China does not feel the need of using physical force to protect himself because he is sure that right and justice is recognized by everybody as a force higher than physical force and moral obligation is recognized by everybody as something which must be obeyed. Now if you can get all mankind to agree to recognize right and justice, as a force higher than physical force, and moral obligation as something which must be obeyed, then the use of physical force will become unnecessary; then there will be no militarism in the world. But of course there will be in every country a few people, criminals, and in the world, a few savages who will not or are not able to recognize right and justice as a force higher than physical force and moral obligation as something which must be obeyed. Thus against criminals and savages a certain amount of physical or police force and militarism will always be necessary in every country and in the world.

...

In fact, what I want to say here, is that the wonderful peculiarity of the Chinese people is not that they live a life of the heart. All primitive people also live a life of the heart. The Christian people of medieval Europe, as we know, also lived a life of the heart. Matthew Arnold says: "The poetry of medieval Christianity lived by the heart and imagination." But the wonderful peculiarity of the Chinese people, I want to say here, is that, while living a life of the heart, the life of a child, they yet have a power of mind and rationality which you do not find in the Christian people of medieval Europe or in any other primitive people. In other words, the wonderful peculiarity of the Chinese is that for a people, who have lived so long as a grown-up nation, as a nation of adult reason, they are yet able to this day to live the life of a child—a life of the heart.

Instead, therefore, of saying that the Chinese are a people of arrested development, one ought rather to say that the Chinese are a people who never grow old. In short the wonderful peculiarity of the Chinese people as a race, is that they possess the secret of perpetual youth.

Now we can answer the question which we asked in the beginning:—What is the real Chinaman[1]? The real Chinaman, we see now, is a man who lives the life of a man of adult reason with the heart of a child. In short the real Chinaman is a person with the head of a grown-up man and the heart of a child. The Chinese spirit, therefore, is a spirit of perpetual youth, the spirit of national immortality. Now what is the secret of this national immortality in the Chinese people? You will remember that in the beginning of this discussion I said that what gives to the Chinese type of humanity—to the real Chinaman—his inexpressible gentleness is the possession of what I called sympathetic or true human intelligence. This true human intelligence, I said, is the product of a combination of two things, sympathy and intelligence. It is a working together in harmony of the heart and head. In short it is a happy union of soul with intellect. Now if the spirit of the Chinese people is a spirit of perpetual youth, the spirit of national immortality, the secret of this immortality is this happy union of soul with intellect.

You will now ask me where and how did the Chinese people get this secret of national immortality—this happy union of soul with intellect, which has enabled them as a race and nation to live a life of perpetual youth? The answer, of course, is that they got it from their civilization. Now you will not expect me to give you a lecture on Chinese civilization within the time at my disposal. But I will try to tell you something of the Chinese civilization which has a bearing onour present subject of discussion.

---

1. "Chinaman" as a term full of stereotypical bias from westerners is here intended, by the author, to be cleansed of the misunderstandings in the stereotypes.

Let me first of all tell you that there is, it seems to me, one great fundamental difference between the Chinese civilization and the civilization of modern Europe. Here let me quote an admirable saying of a famous living art critic, Mr. Bernard Berenson. Comparing European with Oriental art, Mr. Berenson says: "Our European art has the fatal tendency to become science and we hardly possess a masterpiece which does not bear the marks of having been a battlefield for divided interests." Now what I want to say of the European civilization is that it is, as Mr. Berenson says of European art, a battlefield for divided interests; a continuous warfare for the divided interests of science and art on the one hand, and of religion and philosophy on the other; in fact a terrible battlefield where the head and the heart—the soul and the intellect—come into constant conflict. In the Chinese civilization, at least for the last 2400 years, there is no such conflict. That, I say, is the one great fundamental difference between the Chinese civilization and that of modern Europe.

In other words, what I want to say, is that in modern Europe, the people have a religion which satisfies their heart, but not their head, and a philosophy which satisfies their head but not their heart. Now let us look at China. Some people say that the Chinese have no religion. It is certainly true that in China even the mass of the people do not take seriously to religion. I mean religion in the European sense of the word. The temples, rites and ceremonies of Daoism and Buddhism in China are more objects of recreation than of edification; they touch the aesthetic sense, so to speak, of the Chinese people rather than their moral or religious sense; in fact, they appeal more to their imagination than to their heart or soul. But instead of saying that the Chinese have no religion, it is perhaps more correct to say that the Chinese do not want—do not feel the need of religion.

Now what is the explanation of this extraordinary fact that the Chinese people, even the mass of the population in China, do not feel the need of religion? It is thus given by an Englishman. Sir Robert K. Douglas, Professor of Chinese in the London University, in his study of Confucianism, says, "Upwards of forty generations of Chinamen have been absolutely subjected to the dicta of one man. Being a Chinaman of Chinamen the teachings of Confucius were especially suited to the nature of those he taught. The Mongolian mind being eminently phlegmatic and unspeculative, naturally rebels against the idea of investigating matters beyond its experiences. With the idea of a future life still unawakened, a plain, matter-of-fact system of morality, such as that enunciated by Confucius, was sufficient for all the wants of the Chinese."

That learned English professor is right, when he says that the Chinese people do not feel the need of religion, because they have the teachings of Confucius, but he is altogether wrong, when he asserts that the Chinese people do not feel the need of religion because the Mongolian mind is phlegmatic and unspeculative. In the first place religion is not a matter of speculation. Religion is a matter of feeling, of emotion; it is something which has to do with the human soul. The wild, savage man of Africa even, as soon as he emerges from a mere animal life and what is called the soul in him, is awakened, – feels the need of religion. Therefore although the Mongolian mind may be phlegmatic and unspeculative, the Mongolian Chinaman, who, I think it must be admitted, is a higher type of man than the wild man of Africa, also has a soul, and, having a soul, must feel the need of religion unless he has something which can take for him the place of religion.

Study Questions

1. What is the function of defining "Analogism" in the excerpt from the *Mohist Canons*? How does it establish the foundation of the exposition in the following paragraphs?

2. From what perspective does *Han Feizi* explain the "correspondence between actuality and names"? Are there discussions over such a "correspondence" in the other excerpts of this chapter? Compare them with what Confucius philosophizes on "name."

3. Both the *Mohist Canon* and *Gongsun Longzi* mentioned the relationship between "horse" and "white horse." Compare these two. And what does it say about the pursuit of logic for both schools?

4. How do you understand the "moral force" as discussed in *The Spirit of the Chinese People*?

5. In the "Memorial on the Burning of Books," Li Si suggested at the end that "People wishing to pursue learning should take the officials (吏) as their teachers." Please research on the changing of the signified social group of "吏" through Chinese history.

6. The following is a passage from "The Interpretation of Dao" by Han Feizi. Please read and compare the Legalist Dao with the Dao in Confucianism or in Daoism.

The Interpretation of Dao[1]

Han Feizi

Dao is that by which all things become what they are. It is that with which all principles are commensurable. Principles are patterns (wen) according to which all things come into being, and Dao is the cause of their being. Therefore it is said that Dao puts things in order (li). Things have their respective principles and cannot interfere with each other. Since things have their respective principles and cannot interfere with each other, therefore principles are controlling factors in things. Everything has its own principle different from that of others, and Daoist commensurate with all of them [as one]. Consequently, everything has to go through the process of transformation. Since everything has to go through the process of transformation, it has no fixed mode of life. As it has no fixed mode of life, its life and death depend on the endowment of material force (qi) [by Dao]. Countless wisdom depends on it for consideration. And the rise and fall of all things are because of it. Heaven obtains it and therefore becomes high. The earth obtains it and therefore can hold everything. ... Men seldom see a living elephant. They obtain the skeleton of a dead elephant and imagine a living one according to its features. Whatever people use for imagining the real is called form (xiang). Although Dao cannot be heard or seen, the sage decides and sees its features on the basis of its effects. Therefore it is called [in the Laozi] "shape without shape and form without objects." In all cases principle is that which distinguishes the square from the round, the short from the long, the coarse from the refined, and the hard from the brittle. Consequently, it is only after principles become definite that Dao can be realized. According to definite principles, there are existence and destruction, life and death, flourish and decline. Now, a thing which first exists and then becomes extinct, now lives and then dies, or flourishes at first and declines afterward cannot be called eternal. Only that which exists from the very beginning of the universe and neither dies nor declines until heaven and earth disintegrate can be called eternal. What is eternal has neither change nor any definite particular principle itself. Since it has no definite principle itself, it is not bound in any particular locality. This is why [it is said in the Laozi] that it cannot be told. The sage sees its profound vacuity (xu) and utilizes its operation everywhere. He is

---

1. Wm Theodore de Bary, Wing-Tsit Chan, and Burton Watson, *Sources of Chinese Tradition*, New York: Columbia University Press, 1960, p. 260.

forced to give it the name Dao. Only then can it be talked about. Therefore it is said, "The Dao that can be told of is not the eternal Dao."

ABOUT THE AUTHOR

ZHANG TING is an associate professor at the School of English
at Sichuan International Studies University. Her research interests
include English and American literature, comparative literature,
and translation studies. She is also the main participant of the
Chongqing Major Higher Education Teaching Reform Research
Project *Exploration on Teaching Reform of the Experimental Class of
"Chinese Culture Going Global."*